STEAM
The Mystic Harmony

'For the joy of ear and eye,
For the heart and brain's delight,
For the mystic harmony
Linking sense to sound and light:
Lord of all, to thee we raise
This our sacrifice of praise.'

F. S. Pierpoint, 1835-1917

STEAM
The Mystic Harmony

W. Elgar Dickinson

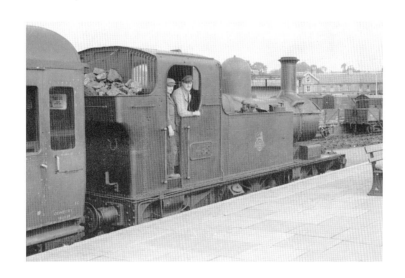

·RAILWAY HERITAGE·
from
The NOSTALGIA Collection

First published in 2009

British Library Cataloguing in Publication Data

A catalogue record for this book is available from the British Library.

ISBN 978 1 85794 328 3

Silver Link Publishing Ltd
The Trundle
Ringstead Road
Great Addington
Kettering
Northants NN14 4BW

Tel/Fax: 01536 330588
email: sales@nostalgiacollection.com
Website: www.nostalgiacollection.com

Printed and bound in the Czech Republic

Half title Returning to Durham University by the Leeds/Harrogate route, I was lucky to capture this 'A3' passing along the up main line, which my train joined at Northallerton. Sadly that Harrogate-Northallerton line is no longer with us.

Page 2 There was a long cinder footpath, the 'Black Pad', adjacent to the Great Central line south of Leicester Central station, as seen from our regular perch on the stile by the end of the garden walls of the terraced houses. In the distance a 'J6' chugs off to the goods yards while a GCR 'Pom-Pom' ambles along with a short freight train.

Title page Footplate crew ready to return to Gobowen from Oswestry. Both men were most affable and delighted to chat with all and sundry on just about any topic.

ACKNOWLEDGEMENTS

S ince this sequel to *A Friend in Steam* was brought about by requests from its readers for a photographical back-up, it is to them that I tender my thanks for having led me to delve amongst my negatives with the consequent delight of reviving multitudes of magnificent memories of the days of the steam-driven railways.

My long hours of seclusion with packet after packet of photographic negatives, with arranging my thoughts, with typing and printing, were most sympathetically accepted by Eluned, my wife. To her go my heartfelt thanks, for without her support and her vital supplies of cups of tea my labours would have become less enjoyable.

Thanks are equally extended to the Editor with Silver Link Publishing, Will Adams, who encouraged me to respond to those requests then supported me with advice.

Any faults of fact, interpretation and dating are entirely mine and attributable to no one else.

Right 'Beware of Trains' – they are addictive! Spotters watch a 2F at a farm crossing near Ratby on the original Leicester-Swannington line.

CONTENTS

DEDICATION

To Mr F. A. Kirk (Fred), that dearest of lifelong friends with whom countless hours were spent in trains and buses, but, best of all, pedalling along thousands of miles of roads and lanes to reach delightful locations at which to exercise the shutters of our steam-dedicated cameras.

And to that 'great and might wonder', as he described himself from an Advent hymn, Dr Wallace Ross, fine musician, cathedral organist, hands-on steam man and inspiration to vast numbers of pupils.

Dr Wallace Ross, more than anyone else I have come across, exemplifies the intelligent, aesthetic, yet mystic rapport between a life spent fulfilling career ambitions while indulging in the fascination of the steam railway. A top-flight musician, successively assistant organist at Gloucester Cathedral and eventually to the full position of organist and master of the choir at Derby Cathedral, Dr Ross also gave himself without reserve to the teaching profession, teaching not only music but also the classics. His devotion to the welfare – spiritual, academic and physical (he took boys on canoeing holidays) – of his pupils was second to none. He was, by nature, a fun-loving man, a characteristic that endeared him to his pupils. Reference was made to this in A Friend in Steam, and he is now enjoying retirement.

During his military service period – in Northern Ireland – his love of the steam railway found a very practical outlet. When free from his duties as RAF Quartermaster he drove steam locomotives for the (Irish) Great Northern Railway, which company was exceedingly grateful. Nor was he employed in the lower grades, proof of which is here, in the photograph he kindly gave me as a schoolboy, showing him proudly standing with his favourite engine *Galtee More*. During school vacations he would be back on the Irish

footplate. His near-countless railway tales delighted all hearers – mostly involving hilarious incidents and characters.

One Eastertide I cycled from Leicester, accepting Wallace Ross's invitation to visit him in Gloucester Cathedral. His superior – Dr Herbert Sumsion – was off duty. My goodness, what an uplifting performance his second-in-command gave the priesthood and congregation on that greatest of days in the church calendar! And I was privileged to be in the organ loft! The close of the service produced an electric rendering of the glorious Bach E-flat fugue – I had always liked it, but this time I was enveloped in it probably as much as Dr Ross himself. I cannot recall my own comment when the last pealing echoes had been wrung from the gorgeous fan-vaulted roof. For his part, Wallace Ross cheerfully commented that, 'The greatest fun on earth is found in only *two* places: in an organ loft and on the footplate of a steam engine!'

Does that not sum up, fully encapsulate, that mystic element in our admiration for the steam engine – provided (this is essential!) that it is balanced by a goodly sense of proportion and a highly worthwhile, self-dedication to contribute, via one's profession, to the world in which we live?

BROADLY SPEAKING

Spiritually, intellectually fathoms below Saint Luke, nevertheless I find myself in a situation similar to his as stated in the opening words of the Acts of the Apostles. That wondrous books opens with the comment:

'The former treatise have I made unto thee, O Theophilus, of all that Jesus did…'

Biblical scholarship has always maintained that, his curiosity being aroused by his reading of St Luke's Gospel (most certainly in a greatly different form from the final, much later version we have today), Theophilus wanted further proofs, evidence of the subsequent doings and work of the Apostles, consequences of the soul-enlightening power of the new faith. He wanted to be updated with the follow-on. The requested, resulting document is exceedingly graphic, piquantly imbued with veracity and conviction.

Likewise your present author, after the publication of his 'former treatise' – A Friend in Steam – has been asked for graphic proofs of what that book described. He realises how greatly he is honoured by such requests and so presents this pictorial selection as graphic support together with a few descriptive words ahead of each section.

Since some experiences in the autobiography were undergone in poor weather, in badly lit environments armed only with basic photographic equipment, there are inevitably several below-par pictures, for which indulgence is sought: at least they illustrate dogged enthusiasm to record occasions possibly unique to the author.

From the outset, work for this predominantly pictorial book was constantly bugged by that acute awareness of the fundamental need to communicate important, personal eye-delighted experiences in all their power, expressed in their complete context. Mere, stark brevity could not achieve this, except in certain instances that will

be obvious to the reader. Like a poet, I told myself, I must *feel* and not only *think* my captions if I am to produce the fusion of sense and sensibility that is the essence of this kind of photographic odyssey. Those who have ploughed through A Friend in Steam will therefore not be surprised by the avoidance when possible of utterly down-to-earth prosaic comments and captions.

Apologies have been offered for poor photographic standards here and there; the thrill of the unexpected, perhaps never-again-to-be-encountered sight was the prime force within my trigger finger as it depressed the shutter release, the figurative fingers of my heart crossed in defiance against the very discouraging lighting conditions or other adverse circumstances.

One and three-quarters of a century ago the French poet, Théophile Gautier, wrote in two prefaces, one to his poetry the other to a novel:

'In general, the moment anything shows itself to be useful, it ceases to be beautiful.'

and

'Being the expression of man's need for something – which is commonly dishonourable – anything useful is thus ugly.'

But the steam railway? Can it be included in the (moral) degradation implicit in this over-simplistic, dubious view? Certainly many landowners and writers of the early to mid-nineteenth century considered it to be a literal blot on the landscape, certainly it brought in its wake ugly slum-building with its concomitant medical and moral diseases. The awesome mushroom clouds from atomic bomb explosions, testaments to the ugliness of such weaponry, are one thing, but the smoke and steam emissions of the steam locomotive are of a different order – they are beautiful despite being evidence of 'something useful' and thus suspect. For steam railway enthusiasts their purely visual beauty counters any suggestion of 'ugliness' – that purposely selfish functioning seen by others as the main characteristic of the railway companies. Didn't we all enjoy above all its other attractions, the *sight* of the working steam engine, for noise, vibration and smell were but magnificent accoutrements, garnishings to the greater mind-grabbing magnificence. The steam railway was pre-eminently the most useful of man's creations. It was indubitably his most beautiful – whence our nostalgia!

As yes, dear old nostalgia! Where would our souls be without it? For the photographer of whatever his hobby might be, there is a doubling of nostalgia's scope and intensity. An example might better explain the point.

As I gaze at a photograph of an A4 topping Stoke Summit my mind fixes upon that for-ever-caught instant, that particular locomotive and its setting. I re-relish the visual awe, re-hear the exhaust, the infamous Gresley 'knock' as I acknowledge the wave from the driver; I recall the passing clickety-click of the coaches, the mixture of early and later BR liveries applied to the mixture of Gresley/Thompson vehicles; the tang of the smoke curdling with an oily wisp. But then, oh then, that photograph serves me further. Hard on the heels of those reminiscences, there surge up under such heady provocation, crowds of memories of the entire day spent by the portals of Stoke Tunnel: the commonplace, the unexpected, the disappointments all form the second layer of the batholithically seated nostalgia. Caught, though not intentionally, in that same photograph stands my wonderful life-long friend. I re-sense his excitement, too, his grin of satisfaction, re-hear his comments. All of the nostalgia speeding through my mind is compounded by further follow-on nostalgia for the innumerable joys shared with him, whether walking the hills, cycle-touring or hunting steam elsewhere. Chatting away on the

Not once did bad weather spoil our joyous days just below the summit of Stoke Bank, a few hundred yards before the entrance to the tunnel. Very exposed to the weather, it could have proved inhospitable, but on the other hand this very openness ensured plenty of full lighting for our photography. For me, this photograph constitutes the totality of the delights of a carefree lineside session. Wonderful, warm weather, the perfume of wild flowers frequently adulterated by the tang of smoke laced with mildly oily, odoriferous steam, delighted the senses. The numerous trains passing before our eyes and through our lenses were unfailingly thrilling, for they either came pounding out of the tunnel or could be heard fighting their way over the last stretch of Stoke Bank, usually giving a whistle to the summit signal box. There was always plenty of time to ascertain the class and its photogenic qualities and ready the cameras, while the

spaciousness of our site allowed us to view the lengthy approach and departure of each train for quite some time – luxury indeed!

But what really makes this particular photograph most cherished by me is not so much the shot of 'A4' *Miles Beevor* but the inclusion of Fred, my marvellous, life-long friend, a companion on countless expeditions to railway sites, on cycle tours and mountain climbs. Here he is wielding one of those excellent cameras made by Ilford, an 'Advocate' 35mm, with superb optics by Dalmeyer.

Every northbound train gave a whistle or a chime as it passed us. What we could not decide was whether the driver was acknowledging us (for some gave us a wave, too) or warning passengers to duck their heads back inside or to close any open windows before the train plunged into smoked-up Stoke Tunnel.

pedal-whirly ride that day to and from home, we refurbished our long-established bonds, one of whose king-pins was the love of the beauty of the steam train. Pedalling off into the homeward sunset with the rewarding glow of contentment with our 'bag' for the day, we would exchange comments and relive it, thereby reinforcing the memory processes, a guarantee for distantly future, powerful, accurate recall and nostalgic delectation – though of course at the time we were totally unaware, ignorant of such psychological mysteries quietly going about their work.

Is it a sign of emotional, intellectual weakness, cowardice in the face of our daily doubts and anxieties, that we seek to lose ourselves in the past? In his masterly play *Les Mains Sales* (*Dirty Hands*), Jean-Paul Sartre, being an existentialist, strongly tends to that view. When a security search is made of the luggage of a young, newly arrived party member – Hugo Barine – at the local communist headquarters, a stash of photographs is found. Shots of Hugo in childhood, sailor suits and all, engaged in juvenile activities provoke a sharpish rebuke from the party leader, Hoederer:

'Why the heck do you want to lug your past around with you?'

Hoederer believes (he is the mouthpiece of Sartre's existentialism) that one must always think in terms of being in a state of 'becoming' – nothing must impinge upon full self-realisation, least of all one's past, which acts as a cloying brake. All right for existentialists, I suppose, but surely the 'pursuit of happiness' depends upon the accumulation of happy experiences, satisfying collections of articles (pottery, books, plants, deepening of religious conviction … railway photographs) for they all, in their various ways, stimulate the desire to move one's life onward via the hobby, in the search for specific goals, quite apart from their value as 'things' to turn to for comfort, for pleasure and aesthetic, intellectual delight. Surely one is entitled to look back on a life that has been of value, whether purely to one's self or to others?

Unhesitating, I therefore offer these nostalgia-provoking photographs. No doubt many may duplicate classes and locations commonplace to everybody. Yet is there not always a tinge of nostalgia when presented by another writer or photographer with a once familiar, long-ago location or locomotive, for I know that I always rejoice to see someone else's picture of a type or place with which I was once acquainted, the location in particular stirring up memories of the occasion when…

What is a railway but a transport system operated by men and women? Having worked with railway folk I was early on cured of the romantic view that the train itself constituted all that was worthy of attention. A section of scenes and the occasional portrait depict some of these utterly dedicated, hard-grinded workers. For me, conversations with them more often than not furnished greater pleasure than the footplates on to which they stepped, the yards that they shunted, the quaint signal boxes that encased them. Not infrequently I was made aware of superior intellects amongst the fraternity, only their 'status', finances, lack of educational opportunity, having barred their way to the higher echelons of trade, professions and government. I have in mind one signalman, a brilliant tenor and flower-gardener with an acute intellect. Had he a degree in horticulture, he could have become a 'Percy Thrower' or maybe, given his superb voice, been trained for operatic fame. Likewise station masters, chief clerks of highest integrity and ability who cared for their underlings, shed masters, carriage-cleaning foremen with like attitudes and abilities to add to their organising excellence. So, as we look at trains, let us never forget the folk who ran all aspects of the railways, day-long, night-through. We enjoyed and photographed the sights, enjoyed the sounds, feel and smells, but they made it all safe and exciting for us.

The saga of my different cameras has been recounted elsewhere. But let us pause awhile to consider their rôle in our hobby. We steam-shooters inevitably regard our equipment as mere dedicated tools, even though at times they are not well-suited to the job in hand. We can become mildly emotional about them. The involvement of a camera with our emotions is simple enough but best explained by an example.

Chased by very chilling winds from a very exposed part of Stoke Bank lineside, I pedalled southward seeking shelter. I ended up on about-to-be-closed Essendine station. Far closer to the track than in my earlier location, I knew that my Ensign Selfix's 1/300-second shutter could not cope with up trains whizzing past at close on 100 miles per hour. It had coped admirably with the ambling freight train from Stamford behind an Ivatt 'C12' 4-4-2T. A porter with time hanging heavily on his hands contrasted acutely with the expresses flurrying about. Eventually, the emotions, the excitement of gazing at the southbound fliers intensified my longing to get shots of them, despite my diminished respect for the sluggishness of Ensign's shutter. I could not help but make a comparison of its lethargy with that of the soon-to-be-unemployed porter. It was not the latter's fault that there was nothing he could do about his situation in the outmoded station. Nor could Ensign be criticised for its current outmoded shutter-speed 'idleness'. But the platform-shaking passage of another streamliner clawed at my emotions and frustration. The next up train was 'pegged'. A distant chime foretold a rip-roaring 'A4'. Gripped by the desire to take back home some record, no matter how blurred, of those whirlwind trains, I pulled out Ensign, focused him up, armed the shutter, his limitations forgotten.

'Well, do your best,' I distinctly recall muttering as I raised the camera.

Now, was that addressed to the shutter or to myself? We were friends again, united in one aim, as it were. Shutter clicked on a gloriously clean Gresley masterpiece. As if to confirm that I had been right at least to have a go, the porter got up from his empty barrow to wander about picking up odd bits of paper – not what he was really wanting to do, but at least he showed willing to make the best of his frustrating situation.

Next I snapped a slightly slower 'A3', though not with much hope of acuity. But I did not care, for my camera was gathering up the equivalent of those bits of paper, my way to overcome my own frustration and disappointment. Those shots have been looked at again, just this minute. That roar, that crashing racket, those smells, that shaking, shimmery livery, that tritonic chime, that porter tackling his despair – all return to thought and heart even as I type, not even distracted by the tempting fresh cup of tea at my elbow. I re-experience a glow of respect for dear old Ensign.

It is only natural that a happy mind imagines a relationship with an inanimate yet always familiar, usually practical object: the favourite walking stick, the seat in the park (your initials adolescently cut into the wood decades ago, entwined with 'hers'), a cherished mug (your companion during many hours of reading over the years). Can these objects, my cameras, exert a talismanic influence, you ask? No! It is merely their essentiality of being the accustomed tool for the job, but more specially, in the case of the camera, the means for the capture and reproduction of the likeness of something admired. It facilitates the recall of past delights. Now pensioned off but cared for, my companionable tools – Penguin, Lumière, Ensign Selfix and Ikonta – are nostalgia arousers in their own right, but, I insist, passively so! Hence, the cut in Ensign's mock-leather covering recalls my dropping it on to sharp gravel when I was in too much of a hurry to change films at Brinklow. The cut material calls forth the first shot on the fresh roll – a 'Princess Royal' on the up 'Merseyside Express'...

So, let us turn over to the pictures! Open up the regulator on the footplate of 'Nostalgia'!

The author 'on the job' approaching Perth in 1960. The locomotive at the head of the train, 'A1' No 60137 *Redgauntlet*, was appropriate since I have been caught 'red-handed', my Bolex D8L cine camera clearly in use! *F. A. Kirk*

1
RAILWAY STAFF

We have always respected, admired, coveted the expertise of steam footplate staff, but yet our attention has primarily focused upon its result – a mind and soul exhilaration of sight, sound, smell and vibration emanating from the locomotives in their charge. References to, and the very rare photographs of these tough, dedicated men thus became relegated to a lower status in books and magazines. Some authors do attempt to establish their utterly vital rôle in the running of the stem locomotive. The likes of R. H. N. Hardy, that hands-on man of steam and evocative relishful writer, refers to footplate staff by name, describes them as real, normal human beings alongside their strenuous labours and dedication. My own acquaintance with those gods of the footplate was regrettably limited to 15-minute conversations in bothies, on the footplate for five moments and from platform ends for still less. But what a grand lot of men they always were!

Yet, far less glamorous though their rôles might be to the passing observer, other equally vital services to the smooth functioning of the railways were in the care of equally specialised, efficient and dedicated men. Who amongst the travelling public gave a thought to the station master, who had to be skilled in countless ways – he was expected to be capable of driving a locomotive should the need arise, organise station staff and their rotas, operate a signal box in emergencies, liaise with countless officers above or below his own status, keep a sharp eye on accounts, encourage local traders to use rail services … the list goes on. The public only came across him in the event of a (very rare) complaint, an emergency or their own special, personal request. Tact, organisational skills and steely courage were his hallmark.

And the signalman, what of him? Merely a bloke pulling levers? Far from it. Your life depended on him. A shunter? Coupling and uncoupling wagons and coaches? Think again of his skills, essential for safety, for the prompt despatch and delivery of goods and passengers. The porter, seemingly lounging around between trains keen on getting tips from passengers? He did indeed merit tips given some of the burdensome tasks he was requested to do by certain kinds of passenger, but when not visible to travellers he would be wrestling with awkward, probably back-stressing articles in the parcels department, he might be frozen stiff at midnight unloading quantities of fish boxes, he could be working desperately unsociable hours in dreadful weather, generally devoid of joyful hours spent with family and friends over Christmas and the New Year in the days of steam. I, as a student, willingly swapped shifts with them over such periods – they longed to be in well-warmed festive family environments while I, impoverished student, desperately needed the overtime pay. But their need was assuredly much greater than mine.

Signal engineers whose task it was to ensure travellers' safety alongside efficient running were an unknown, thus unappreciated body of worthies. Guards, generally taken for granted, at times much stressed by an over-demanding traveller, had to keep themselves on an incessant qui vive. And so the list goes on, from the lonely misery inflicted upon an engine cleaner, the footplate inspector upon whom was laid the responsibility to appoint and upgrade reliable, careful drivers and firemen, through crossing keepers, mechanics, fitters, to engine-shed superintendents – no grade, no labour, no desk job was a sinecure. Let us retrospectively laud them all, respectful of their dedication and expertise, seen or unobserved in the good old days of steam traction.

Like much of the travelling public, I took everything, everyone, for granted along the miles of track along which we sped, but once the railway environment enfolded me within it tentacles there developed within me, unsought, a powerful appreciation of the worth of every grade of railwayman. A perpetual regret, today too remote, nay, impossible to rectify, was the lack of film to record for all time every variety of steam-days railwayman. Here are some of the few that I did manage to capture.

This scene at Chester General really struck my emotions. After shooting the 'Princess Coronation', a clatter from the footplate of the waiting 'Jinty' drew my attention. I expected to see a shovel being wielded. The very young fireman – only in his teens – was gazing longingly at the majestic 'Pacific', whose blower had been put on seconds before, a sure sign of imminent departure. I could 'read' his feelings, his wistfulness, his thoughts of, 'One day I shall fire on the footplate of a top-flight express engine!' Moving to the rear side of the 'Jinty', I believe I managed to capture that mood as well as the setting without pointing the camera, perhaps embarrassingly, directly at the young, keen lad. Doesn't he also call up our own child-time longings to be a driver, or at the very least to have a magical, full-journey ride on a famous class of express engine? Surely you recall the thrusting surge of heartache when, after 'cabbing' a 'King',

an 'A4', a 'Lord Nelson', a 'Princess Royal', you had to clamber down those seemingly huge steps with great spaces between them only to watch the flag-wave from the guard, that white whistle-wisp of footplate acknowledgement, feel the thunder of the opened exhaust, the shudder of the platform beneath your alerted, junior feet, all the time wishing so earnestly to have remained on board! As the nigh-worshipped, loved loco lunged away, your heart went with it until all that remained of the incantatory magic of sight, sound, smell and flesh-stir were their memories. Those hands of yours, now grubby from sliding them down the hand-rails, were sniffed at, even licked – anything to recapture the bliss of the footplate, the searing desire to be roaring along the track, your soul exhilarated beyond any other of earth's experiences as you relished your highly charged, immediately nostalgic imagination!

By far so much more royalist than today, our two preceding generations delighted in naming their offspring after members of the Royal Family. At Leicester Belgrave Road no fewer than four Georges were known to me – maybe more lurked in areas into which my duties never took me. I did make enquiries about name popularity some time after I left the railway. So far as 'George' is concerned, many new-borns were accorded the name when King George V was as yet but the Prince of Wales, but on his accession, after the passing of Edward VII, his popularity soared. The Duke of York eventually, unexpectedly, as our late King George VI, continued the trend. My immediate superior at Belgrave Road Station was a George, though it never entered my head to ask why he had been so named, simply because the naming game held no interest for me. The senior chargehand at Leicester Central carriage sheds was a George, as was the very able chief clerk at the Central station. Given the disparity of their ages, they can probably be regarded as examples of the two historical periods of 'georgification'.

Standing amongst a stack of truly shoddy coal in the tender of a 'J6' 0-6-0 shortly to leave with the un-timetabled afternoon workman's train out of Belgrave Road, I snapped a triumvirate of Georges. The driver and fireman were from Colwick shed and good company when time permitted a chat about just about anything (which included railways, of course!). The guard was a grand fellow, too. Regrettably he was functioning no longer as a passenger guard; arthritis had so crippled his physique that he had been 'withdrawn from moving traffic', as was his phrase. To safeguard his pension he had to remain in railway service until full retirement age was attained. All that could be found for him was carriage cleaning, a hopelessly cruel (though certainly not deliberately so planned) labour for him. He could scarcely wield a brush, and definitely could not carry heavy buckets

of water or, worst of all, manage to clean inside windows with bucket and leathers. He was in excruciating agony on this task. Being fit and relatively young, and a fast worker, I generally did this task for him, though to keep up with appearances and, above all for his own keenly felt self-respect, he nevertheless plodded on as best he could, doing perhaps one compartment to my entire coach. A mine of railway information with a deep well of personal experiences to draw from, he was delightful company, cheery despite his affliction, immaculate despite the dirty facets of the job.

Came the day when, at the Great Central station, he collected his gold watch. He was supremely proud, not of the golden artefact, but of the glowing commendation that accompanied the presentation, girt about with his personal sense of worth having giving of his all, throughout his life, to the railway. We all said our final farewells when he returned. George took me aside and, as a token of gratitude for my extra stints on his behalf, he handed two things to me.

'I want to give this to someone who understands the railway and who will look after it with respect.' He handed me his cherished GNR-stamped brass whistle, a little worse for wear after half a century of use. I declined, knowing how that object was a symbol for him of greater emotional worth than his new watch.

He insisted: 'I shall never use it again, but you might.'

I cherish it as do I also the second thing he insisted I take – his railway war-service badge, 'For over and beyond the call of duty. Thanks for my windows! And thanks for looking after my poorly arms and hands, not to mention my dreadful feet!'

He enjoyed very few years in retirement, passing upward to that superior, happy guard's compartment in the sky shortly before I attempted to make contact with him again when I came down from Wales to visit my family in Leicester.

Above With excitement and expectancy mounting with every train change on our 1954 expedition to photograph Scottish steam, I and my great pal, Fred, recorded incidents along the way. This crew were snapped smiling happily for us with their 'K2' 2-6-0, which shortly rushed us off from Nottingham Victoria to Grantham, and our 'A4'-drawn, late-evening Edinburgh train.

Left The crew of a freight train heading for Grantham glance out at the small assembly of confrères at the end of the eastbound platform of Bottesford ('for Belvoir' says the station board). Shunting was held up by the passage of the 'J39' 0-6-0, allowing the guard and shunter to rest awhile with a quiet cigarette, the shunting pole at 'arms rest'. Footplate staff on the pick-up and shunting 'J6' in the bay were chatting away with the pair until their attention was drawn to the passing freight and its crew. A few words of light banter passed between the sets of footplatemen – a delightful scene illustrating the overall bonhomie so typically enjoyed amongst all grades of railway employees.

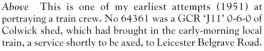

Above This is one of my earliest attempts (1951) at portraying a train crew. No 64361 was a GCR 'J11' 0-6-0 of Colwick shed, which had brought in the early-morning local train, a service shortly to be axed, to Leicester Belgrave Road.

Above right These two very genial fellows would stand and chat with passengers during any lull in their activities at Oswestry. Needless to say, I thoroughly enjoyed my turn

with them. The auto-train run from Oswestry to Gobowen behind their 0-4-2T was lively, with quite high speeds at times despite the short overall distance.

Below A time-honoured branch-line practice is still performed as the guard of the Gobowen-Oswestry auto-train calls out for his passengers descending from the Chester-Birmingham train.

Below This is one of my favourite footplate staff pictures taken on Crewe North shed. While one of the crew of the distant 'Mickey' is oiling round, his mate is chatting with the staff of 2P No 40413. All three of them are looking back at the oil-can wielder. What are they commenting about? The engine, the oiler as a person, or his competence? Is there a serious matter under discussion, or is there a leg-pull in the offing?

Leg-pulling was fairly common amongst footplate men. A tale was told of a fireman recently upgraded from cleaner. Waiting in the shed yard bothy until departure time, his driver asked him to nip on board and shovel a quick round of coal into the box. Keen to do well by showing obedience and willingness, the youngster did so, unaware that a carefully bundled half-dozen fog signals had been left on the 'shovel shelf', as some called it, under a small disguising pile of coal. This was swiftly thrown through the firehole door by the poor innocent. He swung round to reach for a second shovel-load when the most fearful explosion rocked him from behind! The force was insufficient to damage the brick arch or any other part of the firebox, but enough to scare the fireman, who leapt off the footplate, his trouser bottoms smoking, to run to the drivers' bothy, tearfully apologising for having hurled the coal with far too much force, thereby having burst the boiler! I never heard what the drivers' reactions were, but no doubt hearty guffaws rang around the bothy, the tale re-told around that shed and elsewhere for days to come. Or is this an apocryphal tale?

One other fireman-teasing trick, totally danger-free, came to my ears. In one of the former GCR depots way north of Leicester at some time in the late 1930s some fitter or foreman had cut out the base of a worn-out firing shovel, leaving just the sides. For a cigarette or two, he would pass the well-hidden shovel to any driver out for a lark. Out on the line, as often happened, the driver would offer to do a bit of firing, ordering the fireman not to look anywhere but the road ahead while driving. After a few rounds the driver would swap the shovels – the dud having been all the while secreted somewhere – leaving it buried, ready 'filled' for lifting, in the coal pile. When the time came for the fireman proper to resume firing, he would swing round with the empty shovelful while the drive helpfully opened the firehole door! Many and various were the reactions and discussions that ensued, too numerous to list here! Eventually the jape ran its course, all firemen were chary about the shovels, and so the fun ran out of novelty value and died. Where did the shovel, with all the tales it had engendered, end up? It would be interesting to know if some descendant has cleaned it and hung it on his hallway wall...

Below left Sir Henry Fowler, brilliant engineer though he might have been in other spheres, made a dog's dinner of his 7F 0-8-0s. Produced in 1929, they were nicknamed 'Austin Sevens' after the car that appeared the same year, rather as the GNR 'K2s' became known as 'Ragtimers', which music was then also achieving popularity. The axle-boxes, grossly under-engineered, being the same as those of the 4Fs, caused endless failures. Fowler's attempt to produce a better locomotive than the Crewe 'Super D' or some of Hughes's Lancashire & Yorkshire 0-8-0s failed dismally; as new stock, they could not be prematurely withdrawn, so they scorched and wore out countless horns, axle-boxes and the patience of footplatemen and fitters. Here, at Longsight shed, a particularly reprobate class member is given attention by a fitter, one of those utterly vital specialists who literally kept our engines running. Their skills and wealth of experience, not to mention strength, guts, perseverance and preparedness to undertake dangerous work, were worth a fortune to the railways.

Right A favourite cycle amble took friend Fred and me to various parts of the old Leicester & Swannington Railway, sometimes merely for the pleasure of the ride, sometimes with a view to capturing the essence of the line. This scene – Ratby level crossing – typified the line as it had been for decades – a Midland Railway 2F 0-6-0 pulling coal wagons (in this instance return empties) before the advent of the light 2-6-0s and more modern wagons scattered amongst the old wooden ones. So slowly was the line worked that we could gently twiddle our pedals and still beat the lumbering train to each next level crossing.

Naturally, our progress was watched by the railway staff as some sort of light entertainment. Seeing our cameras at the ready, before opening the gates the footplatemen stopped the train short, summoned everybody else forward and stood expectant of their photograph being taken, which we duly did. Passing us to open the gates, the guard invited us to heave our bikes on board and travel to the next set of gates in his van, an offer impossible to decline, of course. The train drew clear of the crossing then stopped to gather up the guard who had closed the gates. We stayed on board until we reached the sidings where the Swannington joined the later-built Leicester-Burton line. We said our goodbyes and thanks, heaved down the bikes, then, to the sound of the steady, lightly smoking chuffs of the 2F, we waved the train and staff on its way.

Somewhat spellbound by the ride and the cheery kindness of the staff, we could not set off home for a few minutes, watching the smoke steadily turn into a darker, more noisome pall as the 2F could be opened up, travelling from here onwards on tracks maintained to the standard required for fast passenger trains. A lovely morning it had been: a wholesome cycle through pleasant country lanes, the allure of the steam railway, the brief yet delightful chat with the railway folk, all set against the sight, sound and small backcloth of the engine and jiggle-clattering wagons. All in all, a perfect ensemble, a harmony that left Fred and me much relaxed, our contentment washed down pleasurably an hour later with a pot of tea.

Below Alf and his alternating shift-mate, Harry, kept the Leicester GNR station signal box in as near brand-new condition as humanly possible. Beyond normal retirement age, they were keen and totally capable of working their box with the utmost efficiency. Both were delightful, highly interesting characters. Here we see Alf and the superbly maintained signal box. More is told of them in my earlier book.

Below Cycling across the town of Bridgwater, Fred and I came to a level crossing without gates. The sight and sound of an approaching train dismounted us and we propped up our bikes. Along waddled '2021' Class 0-6-0 Pannier tank No 2127, born any time between 1897 and 1905 in Wolverhampton Works to the design of William Dean. Interesting though this relic was, the antics at the crossing were more entertaining. Two men leapt off the footplate, one wearing a peaked cap looking as though he was the guard, and the other, more non-descriptively attired, might have been a shunter. Both seemed to want to control what little road traffic there was on just one side of the crossing. The guard more or less ordered his side-kick to cross the road to protect the traffic coming in the other direction. Halfway across, the latter changed his mind and returned to the engine, walking alongside it but not climbing on board. Meanwhile my pal Fred had stopped in the middle of the road (you can see him in the photograph) to watch the train pass. His stance, seeming semi-official, was enough to halt the two cars

approaching from behind him (Fred was completely unaware of this!). The flag-fluttering guard held up cars on his side and the train wobbled its way across the neglected crossing. Once the latter was clear, the traffic started moving (all four cars of it!) and the guard, glancing across at Fred, mouthed a 'thank you!' unnoticed by its recipient, trotted off to climb back on the train, but not without waving his flag furiously in the direction of the footplate. It is safe to assume that he was berating his non-assisting 'assistant' by semaphore!

Bottom Very rarely does one witness a locomotive inspector putting a would-be fireman or driver through his paces 'on the job'. The trilbied, official-looking gentleman had caught my attention when he climbed on to the footplate of the 'D16' in Cambridge station. When he descended a few minutes later, he was accompanied by either the fireman or the driver, of whom he seemed to be asking questions. The would-be driver, moving perhaps from passed fireman or passed driver to full driver, or the equivalent in the case of the other footplateman, was directed to climb down between tender and coach. The inspector bent down to scrutinise whatever was going on. A minute later he returned with the examinee to the footplate. We – the railway club – climbed into the train on the insistent blowing of the guard's whistle. Off went the train. We got off at Ely, but not the inspector, who presumably wanted to see more of his trainee's ability. Let's hope that whoever he was and in whatever grade, he met with the approbation of the inspector. I like this picture on account of its additional subjects: two differently styled water columns, GER and LNER; a glorious array of GER signals and platform lamp; and the distant view of shed activity Variety *was* the spice of observing railway life in those days!

2
PRISTINE PAINTWORK

Always a delight for the eye, any locomotive in sparkling livery was worth photographing as a contrast to the drabness of the common-user policy that inevitably led to neglect, all the more so when it became nigh impossible to attract anyone to what was a filthy, dangerous, unsociably-houred career when cleaner and vastly less physically demanding employment was becoming available, not to mention better pay and swifter promotion prospects. While we gawped and exalted primarily in the noisy magnificence of the passage of a steam train, that wondrous thrilling of our senses could not but be enhanced by gleaming paintwork, super-adorned with brass and copper polished to shimmering perfection. Sadly, such treats were few and far between for many a long year, though at times it seemed that some effort was being applied to appearances so that quite respectable glints and flashes of colour would be enjoyed several times a day. Memories of 1950s visits to the GNR main line are often of perhaps three consecutive expresses roaring past with sparkling engines and stock.

I hold a photograph before me of No 60103 on shed at Leicester where, vilely begrimed, he acquired from the local cognoscenti the polite soubriquet of 'Flyblown Poxman', which remained with him for quite some time. However, still in pre-preservation times, he has gambolled past me on several occasions in his original home GNR territory garbed in clean, polished Brunswick green.

Infrequently, unexpectedly, pristine lowly freight engines might chunter towards us. What, when labour-begrimed, was a shamefully unmanicured, ungroomed, unkempt engine, for once holds our greater attention. We admire the graceful lines of the locomotive – 'No, she's not ugly after all!' Spruced up like some ancient courtesan, she seduces us with her elegantly tarted form. What I would regard as ample support for my contention is the accompanying photograph of the almost straight-from-the-paint-shop, gracious, Gorton-built, svelte GCR 'O4' 2-8-0. Unhappily, a couple of weeks of intense labour among the industrial sites girting Sheffield would greatly diminish her grace, returning her to the status of the diurnal drudge.

After a saddening survey of Gorton's scrapyard, our school railway club marched off to the sheds of the living. Fully expecting to see at least one pristine ex-GCR 'Director' 4-4-0, I was offered only an 'O4' 2-8-0, No 63709, obviously enjoying her first steam-up after a delightful paint-over to round off a major overhaul, the latter proved by her near silent, graceful departure later on.

Above Spotting this gorgeously shiny GCR 'Director' in Sheffield Central from my carriage in the York-Bournemouth train, I risked the latter leaving without me, for I leapt out, coat and camera flailing in the wet wind, sprinted along and snatched a couple of shots. A whistle blew, the guard of my through train was waving his flag, a frantic dash and, wrenching open a compartment door, I reached the one where, in my frenzied excitement, I had left my briefcase and two newspaper-wrapped rounds of cold toast nicked from the college breakfast table 2½ hours earlier. The young lady with whom I had been sharing the compartment from York – she was off to Oxford – quietly asked, somewhat bemused, 'Now what on earth was all *that* about?' Without batting an eyelid I parried, 'As an acquaintance of His Royal Highness, the Prince of Wales, I thought that he might like a picture of one of several locomotives bearing his title.' I was regarded by her two deep blue eyes full of a new respect. Conversation actually was much easier after that, though I did not dare leap up to take any further en route photos, for that would have blown my mendacity into clear daylight.

Left Our guide round Doncaster Works swung us around a corner, flung his arms out and exclaimed, 'There you are, boys – a brand-new engine for you.' We schoolboys gaped at the glorious vision of a brand-new Peppercorn 'A2', No 60139 *Bronzino*. Final jobs were still going on, such as adjusting the safety valves, or so we were told. Personally I thought it rather risky to tackle that task with a full belly of steam right by your head, though the photo does show two men at work by the valves. *Bronzino* was still there an hour or so later, disappointing us that we could not stay to watch this epitome of excellence and beauty make her first wheel-turns.

Right and below Being in the travelling public's eye, N2 0-6-2T No 69537 (*right*) is fully lined out, whereas it would have been wasteful of paint, time and wages to have accorded similar treatment to the otherwise equally well-black-painted 'O2' 2-8-0, No 63976, likely to suffer neglect and nil cleaning once it had left Doncaster paint shop. It would seem essential to further tighten the latter's smokebox door, which is admitting air and allowing exhaust steam to escape, thus likely to create a red-hot door and effectively reduce the locomotive's efficiency (and burning the new paint right off).

Left Although many clean GNoSR 'D40' 4-4-0s had been seen in the course of our 1954 steam-chase around Scotland, Fred and I were taken aback by the splendour of *Gordon Highlander* as he stood in Inverurie Works, his paintwork scarcely dried. No 62277 looked as appealing in BR black livery as he does today in GNoSR colours as a static exhibit. We hoped to see this glory somewhere out on the line in the next few days, gleamingly at work with cleaned coaches, but it was not to be.

Above The old idea of entertaining waiting passengers with gleaming station pilots was revived quite soon by the railways after the end of the war. While scruffy engines were, of course, commonplace, station pilots had the special responsibility of pleading to the public the railways' promise that things were being spruced up, that pre-war standards were on the way back. It was not universally applicable; for various reasons, here and there bedraggled station pilots were on view. Edinburgh Waverley's pilots fitted neither situation; according to several observers, the 'J83s' were maintained in tip-top external condition throughout the war, which meant that, in 1954, what seemed to me to be an exceptionally well-kept locomotive, maybe recently out-shopped, illustrated in fact a decades-long practice that perpetuated a beautiful status quo. No 68473 had a sister who, working the eastern end of the station, gleamed with equal beauty as she moved carriage stock to and fro.

Below Edinburgh Haymarket shed always had an enviable reputation for the superb turn-out of its 'Pacifics' for its prestigious trains. However, second- and third-line locomotives were scarcely ever sent out in a dirty condition. Typical of this pride in their engines is this deliciously sparkling 'V1' 2-6-2T. No 67629 emits an enthralling

display of steam and smoke as she bursts out of The Mound Tunnel with a train for Perth, her Gresley beat laudably audible to our ears, multiplied and thus magnified by the echoes from the stone walls of the Princes Street Gardens cutting – an all-senses-entrancing experience indeed!

Right Fresh from full overhaul in St Rollox Works, 2P 4-4-0 No 40600 waits awhile in Eastfield shed yard before cutting across to St Enoch station to work along the GSWR route. She was utterly beautiful, holding us spellbound as had no other previous sight of an LMS 2P. St Rollox had retained the patterns of the original drawings of these post-1923 engines, for No 40600 sported a true, locally fabricated replica of the Midland Railway capuchoned chimney, a fitting never seen south of the border for decades; we had noticed one or two 3F and 4F 0-6-0s during our Scottish wanderings so fitted. With her more leggy 7ft 0¼in driving wheels, she eclipsed nearby ex-North British 'D30' 4-4-0 *Claverhouse* in graceful raciness, the latter's extra 1,200lb of extra tractive effort failing to restore balance as we compared the two types, the 6-inch-smaller driving wheels counting against the 'Scott'. Naturally, the grimness of the grime-coated 'Scott' also weighed against it. Shortly afterwards, light rain set about bringing down smuts from the heavily smoke-bearing air around the huge shed, spotting the pristine paintwork here and there. Shortly, the 2P snorted out her very own clouds of black smoke, which, in the quickening rainfall, further besmirched her. We rejoiced to watch her move off shed before she resembled *Claverhouse*. Her exhaust was so gentle, like a soughing breeze, while that 'wrolling' sound, typical of southern 2Ps, was totally absent. St Rollox knew something about tolerances and axle-boxes that eluded Derby and Crewe!

Above right Brand-new BR Standard '5' No 73063 looks ready for off in Derby Works paint shop.

Right Super-glinting Midland Railway 3F No 43580 stands in Derby Works paint shop next to a shapely Midland Railway Compound. Although LMSR-built, the 4P can be classified as Midland Railway since it was constructed from spares dating from MR days. We had a well-versed guide with us that day!

Above The school railway club members kindly held back to let me take an unblocked photo of shimmering green 'Jubilee' 5XP No 45606 *Falkland Islands* outside Crewe Works paint shop.

Below A hundred yards further on a likewise glistening 'Princess Royal' stood ready to receive cries of adoration.

No 46201 *Princess Elizabeth* looked quite Swindonian in her Brunswick – ie GWR – green paint. Had Stanier stayed longer with and become CME of the GWR, it is quite likely that a 'Princess Royal' Class would have emerged from his design team, for as early as the late 1920s rumours were running that a 'Pacific' was being mooted in view of the increasing loads with which the 'Kings' might not adequately cope.

Above The first half of the school railway club had reached the bottom of the ramp from the birdcage bridge leading from the station to Crewe sheds and works. In charge of the second batch, I held it back, for an engine was approaching the ramp end. As a result I got a lovely picture of the only freshly painted Garratt 2-6-6-2T I was ever to see. No 47992 was being eased along by an 8F, presumably on shed pilot duty, so probably delivering the monster to Crewe South shed, for which we had been refused permits.

Right Dividing our gang into two batches while on the bridge took a few moments, which were enough to permit a long line of engines newly released from the paint shops to be pushed beneath us by an equally clean 'Austerity' 2-8-0. A 2-6-4T, a 'Black Five' and another 'Austerity' were patently on their way to Crewe South shed. One youngster, who had yet much to learn, tersely commented, 'Why waste paint on them? They're not passenger engines!'

Right Another clean 'Austerity' 2-8-0, the first I had witnessed in years, hauls a huge freight from somewhere north-west of Chester on the Holyhead line.

Above Needing a brief rest during a family cycle tour, we had stopped in Eastleigh for a pot of tea and cake, none of which passed my lips. While the other three were relaxing in the café, I sped off to the nearby sheds. Beyond the lines of engines in generally workaday condition I espied dazzling green locos. Awkwardly placed against the steeply slanting sun, they presented quite a challenge for the camera. A few minutes wandering around sorted out the problems of lighting angles and exposure, and there, in my camera lay pristine examples of a 'Schools' (*Whitgift*) and a 'King Arthur' (*Sir Geraint*). Neither was in steam, but the odour of freshly varnished top-coating required no heat to help its evaporation into an enthusiast's intoxicating balm.

Below Clean 'T9' 4-4-0s were reasonably common in the 1950s, but a sparkling fresh-from-the-paint-shop beauty was a delight indeed, and so unexpected, as I 'bunked' Eastleigh shed. It was sporting the partially lined-out mixed-traffic black livery that was not always to been seen on other class members, presumably because of financial restrictions. Memories rose up as this loco recalled Southern Railway-liveried specimens in pre-1948 days, only one looking smart, however. The extended smokebox I had disliked ever since seeing pictures of 'T9s' in original condition. 'Paddleboxes' and other 'nose-heavy' LSWR engines also met with my disapproval so far as looks were concerned, but the more I read of the prowess of the 4-4-0 classes the more my disapprobation of them diminished, but not so in the case of the pretty well unsuccessful Drummond 'T14' 4-6-0s. Somewhere I have a negative of one of those monsters passing Clapham Junction in 1950; I was in the company of a few photographers who persuaded me it was worth shooting.

3
FAVOURITE SPOTTING SPOTS

'It makes the wounded spirit whole
And calms the troubled breast
'Tis manna to the hungry soul
And to the weary, rest.'

John Newton, writing this wonderful hymn in mid-eighteenth-century England was quietly exulting in the happy, restorative powers of the Christian's genuine, spiritual experiences. There was nothing fanciful about it. It was, always will be, indeed wholesome, strength-giving and curative, encouragingly satisfying. Beyond its statement of faith that verse contains a psychological truth applicable to other life experiences:

Lose yourself in something beyond yourself, greater than yourself, and you will gain mental and spiritual refreshment and encouragement. Hobbies, sport, quality music, ballroom dancing, painting, study – all these and more besides (if they are taken up in a non-superficial way, which would soon pall) – will so take one's mind from its troubles, from its lack of calmness, from the hurts it has endured, that when one has to return to these vexations, the refreshment from the hobby gives hugely added energy and a greater sense of proportion, of perspective, to the mind and soul, enabling one to cope with greater calm and assurance. We all need our 'bolt-hole', our 'shed at the bottom of the garden'. But these have to be of excellent quality and capable of taking us out of our problems, making the walk down the path to them worth the effort. ('Oh take me out of the mire that I sink not!' pleads the psalmist, wallowing unwillingly in his woes.)

The railway enthusiast, and the steam photographer in particular, found a first-class source of mental recuperation, of recharging the batteries, of losing one's self within a different world, a bigger world. One of the countless advantages of steam-watching, of steam-chasing,

was the inexhaustible number of locations available, even if finances never stretched sufficiently to get everywhere. Eventually there was always a within-reach set of favourite spots, which, when attained, exuded sights, sounds, smells and vibrations that were 'manna to the hungry soul'. If the journey was longish and difficult, the weather against one, once settled by the lineside the watching of trains came as 'to the weary, rest'.

Even without a desperate need for solace and mental refurbishment, such sorties never failed to refresh and cheer for days to come. It was never out of mere habit that I and companion(s) ended up at favourite spotting spots. We went to them because they were especially suitable for viewing, for photographs, delightful in themselves and, of equal importance, because they were reached only after delicious cycling along lovely lanes, or even main roads, provided the scenery was attractive. Added to the enticement of wondering what we might see was the spice of the journey itself. I have written elsewhere about the pleasure of pedalling along leafy, wildlife-loaded lanes to Brinklow, to Stoke Summit, to remoter parts of my local GCR line, the thrills of cycling late evening with a gently humming dynamo accompanying the profound pleasure of a quality friend's voice. We appreciated it all: a great day by the lineside, cameras clicking away, eating simple good food, relishing the muscular efforts demanded by the ride, the heart subconsciously singing during the return trip in echo to the fifteenth-century Latin hymn, 'Oh let the heart beat high with bliss'!

Perhaps the steam railway past has so faded for many that, as a hobby, like the biblical salt, it 'has lost its savour'. Has memory lost its tangy salt, too? Favourite spotting spots have gone, have been transmuted beyond recognition, preventing the easy recall of past steam excitements. I stated earlier that the railway photographer has quite an advantage in such circumstances. He can pull out his photographs taken precisely where he obtained utmost enjoyment, refreshment, rest, all those decades ago. For me, my photographs are my salt-cellar. Let me sprinkle some in this chapter!

Above Seen from the down platform at Brinklow, north of Rugby on the Trent Valley line, a 'Patriot' approaches the station with an RAF personnel train. The signal box, a train waiting in the loop and a still serving goods yard add interest to what today is an empty stretch of line.

Below Looking north, an up Liverpool express tears through. This view shows Brinklow to have been a typical LNWR country station with its tunnelled stairways, oil lamps and simple passenger shelters. The booking-hall-cum-waiting-room is built above the tracks. Smoke, steam and a tremendous racket readily penetrated this area, no doubt to the consternation of timid travellers. In its last years the only window was jammed open and eventually broken, increasing the unpleasantness. No wonder the public deserted the local service!

Right Once Brinklow station was closed, our alternative and preferred spot was a quarter of a mile up the canal towpath. With a beautiful exhaust display – and well cleared out of the driver's vision, unlike that of the 'Coronations', which needed smoke defectors – a 'Princess Royal' roars up to us with a Manchester express.

Right A respectably clean 'Patriot, No 45505 *The Royal Army Ordnance Corps*, takes on the lowly yet money-making duty of a freight working, passing northwards.

Below In the days of numerous named trains – always a good publicity aid – rebuilt 'Patriot' No 45540 *Sir Robert Turnbull* swoops down the grade with a very long and well-packed 'Mancunian'.

Above Later, under the new steam's-doom-threatening catenary posts near Brinklow, a 'Princess Coronation' hurtles London-wards, her smokebox reporting board hiding her identity.

Below A 'Princess Royal' charges up the slight grade beyond Brinklow station with a Liverpool express. During a day spent by the lineside, a large proportion of up and down Liverpool trains was in the hands of this class.

Atherstone almost equalled Brinklow as a favoured location. Perhaps it was the more beautiful, more scenic, quiet lanes route to Brinklow that tilted it in our favour. The cycling to Atherstone took us along main roads all the way, though we would get compensating glimpses of trains on the Leicester to Nuneaton and Birmingham line, and, with a spot of luck a good view of the traffic along the Nuneaton-Coalville LNWR&MR joint line over which we passed.

Atherstone station was – still is – a fine example of 'stately home'-style architecture, possibly so planned on account of the country gentry who would descend there to participate in the famed Atherstone Hunt; they would expect a station worthy of their personal status, so, Jacobean it had to be.

Rudely contrasting with it was the high-perched signal box, which would disappear in wreaths of smoke at the passing of most trains. The point and signal rodding added to its spindly look, while giving us visual and audible advance warning of any approaching train, the expresses sending tremors through the box as they roared beneath it. It was surely a most arduous box to work, train frequency being not far from non-stop.

In these views No 46100 *Royal Scot* scorches southwards with a great length of carriages from Glasgow (*above*), and, looking south, the down 'Royal Scot' train is drawn by 'Coronation' Class No 46244 *King George VI*.

Back home in Leicester there was a long, narrow cinder footpath behind a street of Victorian terraced houses, presumably built for Leicester's railway employees of the Great Central Railway who would be at work in the nearby large goods yards, warehouses and their associated office blocks, to the south of which lay the engine sheds. It was a marvellous spotting spot (see also page 2), with a wide choice of viewpoints from which to enjoy the shunting, engine manoeuvres in the shed yard, the regular passage of freight and passenger trains, expresses and locals – enough to keep any spotter content for hours.

These two views typify what could be seen at almost any hour of the day at the north end of the path. Ex-ROD 'O4' Class No 63772, just uncoupled from its up freight, is making for the loco shed for servicing. Once cleared, it is replaced by 'J52' 0-6-0T No 68839, which sets about dismembering the train formation, taking anything up to a couple of hours to complete the task, as to the variety of sidings is added the lengthier trek to the warehousing complex. The shunters were men of endurance and skill, a delight to watch as they separated (or 'cut', in their parlance) arrivals or made up departing traffic.

Above North of Werrington on the East Coast Main Line is the level crossing at Lolham. Never have I seen other spotters there. The gates were exceedingly wide given the number and spacing of the railway tracks, their opening giving us ample time to prepare for photographing whatever came along. The footbridge offered an alternative position for photographs. Broad, grassy roadsides made comfortable seating for us when rail traffic lessened or our cycle-ride provoked our appetites for a replenishing and relaxing snack.

My life-long cycling, hiking and steam-adoring pal, Fred, captures with his Leica camera a slow-moving up mixed freight behind a 'K3'.

Below Thundering north through Lolham comes *Flying Scotsman*, dressed in his ultimate BR frills of double exhaust and German-style smoke deflectors. My, he sounded in fine fettle as he faced the start of the long haul up to Stoke Summit!

Above Was Grantham station and its vicinity ever devoid of trainspotters? I doubt it. I loved the place. 'Songs of praise then let us sing! Alleluia!' – one expected songs of praise to ring out whenever *Mallard*, illustrious *Mallard*, put in an appearance, which was quite often. He is in charge of the up 'Tees-Tyne Pullman', known to most spotters by the obvious nickname 'Tea-Time Pudding'.

Below My move from the Midlands to North Wales severed me from my favourite haunts along the GNR main line and from beautiful spots like Brinklow. A tough 90-minute cycle

ride from my home in the Clwydian Hills would take me to a deserted stretch of Gresford Bank. The effort was well rewarded, for the demands of the up-line gradient guaranteed magnificent sights and sounds from pounding engines while, unless the ears were alert, descending trains with steam shut off could creep up and pass the unprepared cameraman. Here are two shots depicting this contrast.

In the first, a thrashed 'Castle', No 7019 *Fowey Castle*, rattles the windows of closed Gresford station on the final stretch of the tough southward climb, my scalp garnering quite a collection of cinders as she passed...

Above ...while on the down-grade a cleaned-up 'Hall' fails to sneak past me unphotographed with its immaculate Birkenhead train.

Below A reasonably easy cycle ride would frequently bring me to the lineside on the cinder track by the outlet of Wrexham's Croes Newydd shed. With a level crossing hard by, advance warning of any movements and passing trains was most helpful. Occasionally a train would take a run at the steeply graded line to Brymbo steelworks, passing the sheds and myself. This line is seen diverging on the right-hand side of this photograph of a local favourite, '73XX' 'Mogul' No 7339, passing the shed outlet with an all-stations from Shrewsbury.

Above It was not long before equally absorbing delights were found in and around Chester City. What a superb observation location! Immediately south of Chester General station all was former LMSR territory, with its main line to London and another to Manchester, together with the immediacy of the loco shed to spice the joys of the location. The occasional ex-GWR loco might sneak into the shed yard for coal and water, but would never go on shed. I was kept on my toes by the almost constant arrivals and departures of passenger trains, of through freights and of light engine manoeuvres. I was merely an observer, whereas the signalmen in the nearby box must have led a frantic life. Two freights, behind an 8F and a 4F, remind us that this traffic was the main source of income for the railway companies. Now, just have a look at the still-extant and functioning ex-LNWR signals in 1960! My wish

to snap a 'Super D' beneath them to create a period piece was never granted. Since these 0-8-0s lacked smokebox number plates, who could have decided when the picture might have been taken – LNWR, LMSR or BR period?

Below Given my fitness, long walks from Chester station to the City Walls, and beyond to the Golf Club cutting, were no problem. There were always surprises laid on for anyone sitting opposite Chester Golf Club: two main lines, the GWR south to Paddington and the LNWR north-west to Holyhead, guaranteed variety, while traffic on the Chester-Ruthin branch and the proximity of Mold Junction shed produced unexpected extra delights. Primarily a passenger-train engine, an ex-LMS 2-6-4T hauling a lengthy hopper train northwards was indeed a rare working worth recording.

4
INDUSTRIAL STEAM

There was a time when almost any railway journey would pass by or through industrial complexes, some diminutive, some massive. Heavy industries – iron foundries, steelworks, pottery works, large-scale quarries, collieries, for example – ran their own internal, complex railway systems on quite a large scale. Even into the 1950s such systems were still to be seen during my regular travels northwards through the Midlands. Annoyingly, they were nigh impossible to photograph for one reason or another: modern and quaint old motive power could be glimpsed skulking behind lines of wagons, or they might be penned in beneath metal-sheeted roofs, cut in half by low-level power-lines, girders and so on. Consequently I scarcely bothered to have the camera ready, accepting to observe and enjoy their fussing activity. Smaller industries, requiring far fewer sidings by virtue of what they manufactured – industrial locomotive builders, for example – were no less frustrating. Once supplies of coal and sheet/tube metal had been delivered to the works, the one or perhaps two works engines would be parked out of sight or too far away for the camera.

It was possible to visit ironstone quarries, to enjoy their fascinating variety of locomotives and wagons, but with so many other demands on my time – not to mention money – I never indulged in seeking them out.

What few photographs I did take were mainly by chance. Only one of this brief selection was taken from a moving train, while one other happened to be around when I was set on seeing the famed *Cecil Raikes* at work. The rest were encountered while pursuing other goals.

Cycling to my fiancée's home in Aberdare, I was fortunate to spot these two, *Sir Gomer* on the left, pootling around with coal wagons in Pontypridd, scruffy and sounding fit to disintegrate.

Below After 'bunking' Sunderland shed and drying out after a storm, I wandered down to the quayside and harbour. To my great delight along trundled two entrancing locomotives: a mobile crane and a Pecket 0-4-0 tank. Once snapped, they disappeared along the quay and were lost to sight, never to return that day. Had they gone on shed somewhere or what? All I knew was that my arrival had been accurately, though undeliberately timed that morning. Talk about good luck!

Bottom A bitterly icy day in January was not ideal for cycling around the Leicestershire and Nottinghamshire wolds, but a friend and I were keen to visit the decrepit Waltham-on-the-Wolds branch, then seek out what we could of the still more decrepit Eastwell Iron Quarries lines with their strange ways of working, way up in Nottinghamshire's portion of the wolds.

'Snow was falling, snow on snow, in the bleak mid-winter' sings the traditional carol, and, my goodness, how we soon experienced it in ample measure. Having set out with a specific aim, we were in no mood to call it off, so struggled manfully, or should I say 'teenagefully', up to the plateau, frozen to the core. Nothing moved anywhere, all was desolation. Crunching our wheels through frozen snow along a vague trackway, we came across this sorry, abandoned 0-4-0 saddle tank, bearing the appropriate name of *Scott*, to which, with uniform spontaneity, we added 'of the Antarctic'. The sullen afternoon sky, scowling still more darkly as we peeled off gloves to make use of our cameras, obliged us to take hand-held, slow-speed-shutter shots. Not a good photo, but worthy of consideration for it contains examples of the tipper trucks and a loading crane, all of considerable vintage, while for me personally it encapsulates what steam-chasing is about. Good healthy exercise rewarded by the chance to study and record something about which one has read, something that has played a great rôle in the economic development of a particular part of the country, something that was designed and built to suit the requirements of that industry, taking into account geological factors, such as terrain and what it consisted of – the list can be longer.

Despite near-frostbite and exceeding tiredness, we exulted in the success of our wanderings, in the acquisition of fresh on-the-spot knowledge, no longer just armchair reading. Importantly, we felt further impulses towards that vital self-respect that grows steadily in teenagers when challenges are set and met – some 'mystic harmony' here between demanding activity, reading and self-awareness, surely wrought by the happy provocation of studying steam railways!

Opposite top and middle Way back in 1950, with my primitive camera slung around my neck, the annual family cycle tour headed for the Welsh Borders. Just past Atherstone I spotted a most strange-looking locomotive a very long way off on the ex-LNWR main line. I just could not make out what it was, but took a hopelessly distant photo. Despite a massive degree of enlargement it remained a blurry, utterly unresolvable mystery, its shape impossible to delineate.

It remained forgotten until 1962. That was the year when I cycled from North Wales to South Wales (via Leicester to call on my parents) to spend time with my fiancée. Trundling downhill I saw smoke in the distance, to my right. Funny, I thought, the LNWR is on the left. As I drew nearer the bottom of the hill, so did the smoke. I crossed the unprotected level

crossing, dumped the bike and expectantly hauled out my camera, the 1950s incident still dormant, unaroused in my mind. Within half a minute along chuffed a beautifully compact Beyer-Garratt 0-4-4-0 with a trail of coal wagons. Only then did that old experience leap with new clarity into my mind. 'So, I had been right all along! There *was* a strange engine! I was not seeing things!'

A mile or so away was Baddesley Ensor Colliery, whose servant this Garratt was, running fetch-and-delivery errands between the mine and the LNWR line. Taking my time, I made most sure of recording the full beauty of this vision, firing away a good half-dozen rounds from my film-stock cassette at her in retaliation for the disappointing, frustrating defeat she had inflicted upon me twelve years earlier.

Bottom As described – and illustrated – in *A Friend in Steam*, one of my cycle epics took me to the NCB collieries at Heanor to hunt down *Cecil Raikes*, the former Merseyside Railway outside-framed 0-6-4 condensing tank engine. That goal achieved, attention was turned to seek out anything else of interest. The first 'anything' was a superbly maintained, Caledonian-blue-painted 0-6-2T, No 41, working the colliery sidings, and here he is. I wondered at the time whether the trailing four-wheel truck of 'Cecil' had impressed the original colliery owners, for its guidance around sharply curved sidings stopped the driving wheels from spreading the track. Did that lead the owners to supplement their motive power with something similar? Anyone know?

My second 'anything' was the unexpected arrival at long-closed Heanor station of an enthusiasts' excursion hauled by a cleaned-up GNR 'C12' 4-4-2T. The platform was just about empty, for the overbridge was filled with camera-toting folk. Needless to say, I joined them and took a snapshot that must have been replicated by several hundred others, since we all occupied the same few square yards of roadway and bridge. I have yet to see any of them, however. Vexingly, that negative is one of the very few that have been mislaid over the years, surprising me greatly since several negatives of *Cecil Raikes* and of other shots that day are all safe and intact. Happily I have one print made from it. Did I lend the negative to some forgetful soul?

5
SHOT FROM THE TRAIN

'Shout as ye journey on,
Songs be in every mouth;
Lo from the North they come,
From East and West and South.'
C. E. Oakley, 1832-65

Mr Oakley lived through the earliest years of steam railway transport. How delightful it would be to learn that he had lived in London within reach of all the termini to which he would go to watch the arrivals of trains from every point of the compass, rejoicing in the excitement! And did he perhaps delight in making many a train journey in a variety of directions – both subliminal inspirations for his Christian hymn? What fanciful thoughts, indeed! We of the twentieth and twenty-first centuries most certainly have covered much mileage by train, coming and going along a host of compass bearings, be it for business or pleasure, and, as steam enthusiasts, sticking our heads and cameras out of windows. Name me an enthusiast who has never so behaved!

In the company of a fellow enthusiast, we would station our separate selves one on either side of the corridor-end door windows, to share the look-out responsibility. We did indeed 'shout as we journeyed on':

'Quick! An "A4" coming! I'll try and get a shot out of the next door-light. You come here!'

And across one would stride to take up a hurried stance with camera armed, focused and held steady.

'Did you get it? I got a super shot – I think. Yippee! It was *Bittern*, one I've wanted to see for ages!'

Songs of sorts were in our mouths as we gloated over a successful snap taken of an express 'from the North'.

Not so long ago best pal Fred and I spent a day travelling around the Severn Valley Railway. Cameras around necks, we stood at dropped windows and whooped as we spotted and snapped the preserved 'Dukedog'. I noticed Fred brushing a speck or two of ash from his hair. I got a mildly wetted collar, thanks to the fringe spray from the fireman's pep-pipe on the 'Duke'. We slightly changed our tune for a few seconds, fearing lest dust or moisture had settled on our precious cameras.

Generally speaking one had a good idea of what to expect on boarding a train. Travelling to Durham so frequently from Leicester, most of the exciting locations were eagerly awaited, despite the foreknowledge of exactly what class of motive power would be found there. Selecting alternative routes undoubtedly increased the variety, but even then it was rare indeed that the unexpected passed before the camera. I could travel via Derby, Pontefract and York, or Derby, Harrogate and Northallerton, or Rugby, Carlisle and Newcastle and so on, each route eventually becoming well established in my memory together with its regular studs of motive power. However, I was never bored for a second by the repetitious routes, for every location I passed through, every engine I saw was like an old friend, a delight to meet again, some being photographed on several different occasions.

But what about holidays? Now, here we enter quite a different situation in which novelty plays a superb rôle. Travels to the continent introduced me to classes never seen before on the ex-Southern Railway lines, one special instance being the chance to photograph two side-by-side 'R1' 0-6-0Ts, one with standard boiler mountings but the other with much reduced ones to enable it to work through the narrow-bore tunnel on the old Canterbury & Whitstable branch (see Chapter 6). Infrequent cycle-tour-time-saving trips in the West Country presented me with ex-GWR and ex-Southern Railway sites and engines, all keenly looked out for as I travelled 'From East and West and South'.

Exceedingly infrequent were my journeys to London, but when heading so far south my camera was scarcely inside the windows. I expected the unexpected to be passed in sidings, passing loops, at junctions and stations. An engineer's train with its codicil of an ancient coach gave me much pleasure, for it had been spotted trundling some way ahead on the slow line. Plenty of time was available to stare at it as we drew past, before the clean 2P 4-4-0 up at the front end became the

recipient of my eager studying stare, the entire train then snapped by my faithful Ensign Selfix camera.

Close on a quarter of my negatives owe their existence to being exposed from a moving train. Some of them, for a variety of reasons, are abominably poor, but have been retained as memory agitators. Others I personally regard as quite respectable, and some of them are reproduced here.

Not long out of London Victoria station I met an ex-SECR Class 'C' galloping along with a passenger train – unless it was on mere carriage pilot duties for that station. Subsequent sightings on my way to Folkestone showed that the class was still fundamentally serving as freight engines, just one other being spotted on a passenger duty.

Left Before the advent of 'Britannias' and the occasional 'Royal Scot', expresses out of St Pancras were invariably drawn by 'Jubilees'. One such typical departure from the elegant terminus was taken from my shortly-to-follow slower train behind a 'Black Five'.

Below Once the preserve of unrebuilt, unsuperheated 2P No 40383 and just one 'Jinty', Derby's carriage sidings were worked by a trio of 'Jinties', though on odd occasions other motive power stepped in to cover for an absent-for-repair 0-6-0 tank. My regular journey from Leicester to Durham always began around 7.00am, which brought me past the Derby sidings around the time the movement of carriage stock was under way. One morning the 'Jinties' were somewhat tardy; instead of seeing them busily making up formations or towing some stock station-wards, I was treated to the vision of them scurrying along, coupled up. The White Rabbit's anxious exclamation in *Alice in Wonderland* came to mind: 'I'm late, I'm late, for a very important date!'

Right This 3F was caught running past the site of the old ticket platform east of Derby. I well recall the days when what seemed to be in interminable hold-up was in fact an essential procedure to prevent dishonest travellers from 'bilking' the then LMSR. Very rarely, heated voices along the corridor disclosed the apprehension of an offender. Any refusal to pay up immediately brought a railway police officer from the platform to arrest and remove the obdurate rogue; this I never witnessed, but was told about it by my father.

Below Signals, especially complex gantries, were always fascinating for steam-watchers, both as attractive in their own right and, more importantly, as harbingers of soon-to-appear trains. The gantry by Derby North box consists of standard LMS equipment. I have memories of the days when it bore beautiful Midland Railway arms. I liked to attempt composite photos from time to time, so here I portray the Midland box, some of its signals and a 3F approaching with a freight train. What a pity the pre-1923 arms were not still in place, to give me what would have been a completely Midland Railway period depiction.

Left The only truly successful compound-cylindered engines were those introduced in 1903 on the Midland Railway. Eventually, as a result of the 'Midlandisation' of the LMS shortly after its formation, well over 400 of them sere scattered across the company's routes, thereby earning them the soubriquet of 'Crimson Ramblers'. No 40931, one of the 1924 LMS-built examples, is caught passing through Duffield on its way to Sheffield.

Below Somewhere just north of Sheffield this open view of a goods yard with two engines appealed to me as typical of freight pick-ups and depositings. A 3F and an 8F are busy, the former engrossed in the shunting and latter waiting to set off with the goods.

Right The massive engineering of the tunnels and cuttings just beyond Sheffield is awesome. The smoke, the noise, the alternating of tunnel, air-shafts and deep, walled cuttings make for a difficult photographic choice. Several attempts were disastrous failures, but perseverance was rewarded on this one occasion. It is hoped that the majesty and magnitude

of the works have been captured together with the depiction of the 'Black Five' and train struggling up the grade. Now, who is the fellow taking a risky walk along the track on the right? What is he doing?

Below When catching the 7.13am from Leicester Midland I had to change at Derby for a York connection on my way to Durham. The delights of this route continually unfolded, for there was so much to see. A sharply keener sense of anticipation would arise when I saw we were getting close to Rotherham. Here I expected to be welcomed by a dear old faithful friend. Always parked in the same spot, never well lit so early in the day, ex-Midland Railway, open-cabbed, her round-topped boiler crowned with Salter spring balanced safety valves, 1F 0-6-0 No 41835 lit up my mind, for she was the very last of her kind, and surprisingly long-lived (born in 1878). As we slowed down to stop at Rotherham, the lovely loco was photographed from the rear expressly to portray the open cab and safety valves. This is the most successful photo of the half-dozen or so attempts taken over the years – the early hour of the day, much smog from local heavy industry and pouring rain always seemed to take their turn in thwarting me. This time I was in luck – just enough light and no obfuscating atmospherics. A brick hut in which the 1F's crew presumedly rested and lunched still stood, albeit decrepit and near tile-less, when quite recently I passed the nostalgia-evoking site.

Top Although the 'J72' was interesting enough a subject as it filled its tanks, my purpose was to record the old Midland Railway roundhouse at York, due for demolition. The next time I passed, the water crane still stood but all that remained of the shed was a small, forgotten pile of bricks.

Middle Always on the qui vive for the unusual, my head was not a little chilled as I was hustled south across the Great Plain of York at Raskelf by *Owen Tudor*, a Thompson 'A2'. I was about to withdraw in anticipation of a hot cup of tea at York when something was perceived heading northwards. It was a Thompson 'K1', a type of which I already had several shots. Just at the last moment I spotted men standing upright in one of its trailing wagons. Further out again went my head, and out came the camera just in time to snatch a photo of an engineer's train and record the poor frozen devils. I waved as we passed at a combined speed of over 100mph. Hanging on for grim life, they could only acknowledge me with a vigorous nodding of the head. Now what game was afoot there? Was it a stupid wager, some unusual experiment, or what?

Bottom Before joining the electrified line from Manchester into Sheffield, my 'B1'-hauled train has been slowed by signals. Again, popping my head out to see why proved fortunate, for an ex-GCR 'N45' suddenly swung into sight. I had taken static shots of this class elsewhere, so this was my first chance to record one actually moving. As always, my Ensign Selfix camera was at the ready – a quick focus check and the shutter was fired.

Opposite top left Ex-GCR No 67439 belonged to the earlier, 1903, 'C13' Class of suburban tanks. Very few remained in service when I was blessed with this sighting just outside Sheffield, running light-engine beneath the wires of the eventually scrapped electrified Manchester-Sheffield trans-Pennine route. We could well do with its reinstatement these days when the alternative Midland route, we are told, can scarcely cope with its traffic.

Opposite top right Hopes of travelling with the school railway club behind an ex-GER 'J15' from Kettering to Cambridge were unrealised – an Ivatt Class 4 was our motive power. The disappointment was amply cancelled when we crossed paths with a

Cambridge-Kettering train at Thrapston. The slight curve ensured that I included not only the desired 'J15' but also our Ivatt.

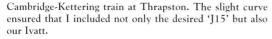

Below 'J39' 0-6-0s being rarities on the ex-GCR lines south of, and perhaps including, Nottingham, this sample just had to be snapped in dear old Nottingham Victoria as I leaned out

of the York-Bournemouth train. Just look at the length of the train – using it on average four times a year, I had never known it sparsely occupied, let alone to be run, even in winter, with fewer coaches. Beechingisation robbed the travelling public of this highly convenient through service from the North East to the South Coast, picking up and depositing customers at myriad towns and cities en route.

Above Time was running out on one particular cycle tour, and at least one day could be gained by a train ride. My bike, stacked on board at Basingstoke, was heaved out at Reading to be deposited in a cavernously empty guard's van on an all-stations train to Oxford, though I was due to descend at Goring & Streatley. The 'Castle' at our head was churning the miles past, but not far short of Goring up on the left charged a sister engine. What excitement to be travelling

around the 70mph mark with a clean 'Castle' moving at one's side at perhaps an additional 10mph. Mesmerised, I studied that shapely masterpiece with particular attention to the coupling rods and wheel revolutions, perfectly synchronous with the perfectly regular exhaust beat (valve settings were patently first class – well done, shed fitters!). The overall sound, so close and for seemingly so long – probably under a minute – was exhilarating. Hearing, vision, intellect and the aesthetic sensibilities were wonderfully co-ordinated as if by some sympathetic magic.

Below left On the one occasion when the sun shone for me during a farewell trip along the Ruabon-Barmouth line, I was delighted to take this 'double-yoker' photo (as two-for-the-price-of-one shots used to be called) at Glyndyfrdwy. My BR Class 4 waited for the Standard Class 5 to drift in with its train from Barmouth. For a few minutes the drivers of both trains were in conversation, though about what I could not discover, being too far away. My train waited until the other had completely cleared the station. Nothing untoward was apparent throughout the rest of the journey, so perhaps the chat had been about something personal – or had they been placing bets on the horses running in Chester Races that afternoon? Your guess is as good (or bad) as mine!

Top Saltney Ferry Junction, alias Mold Junction, was always eagerly looked forward to for it was right next to Mold Junction shed, with its air of intense activity and variety of freight engines. It was also the dropping-off and picking-up station for a large number of footplate and other shed staff, with whom I engaged in happy little chats from time to time.

Middle This up freight behind a BR Standard 'Mogul' drew my attention from shed-watching at Saltney Junction.

Bottom As my Ruthin-Chester train neared the portals of the short Chester Tunnel I was treated to the magnificent sight of a BR Standard Class 5 charging up the grade with a fast fitted goods destined for places along the Holyhead line.

A regular broad vista for me, including here the Ruthin-Chester train, was ever-bustling Mold Junction shed. It never disappointed, except that every engine I saw was in an incredibly filthy state, apart from one particular Saturday when I spied a pair of respectably looked-after machines.

These two locomotives deserved to have their portraits taken as an example of 'the exceptions that prove the rule'. One is an 8F 'Consolidation' – known to us all, of course, as 'Consols' – and the other is a 4F. Perhaps I should have endeavoured to read their shedplates, for though dirtied they certainly did not match the eternal deep grubbiness of Mold Junction's stock.

6
SERENDIPITY

Until recent years 'serendipity' was a rarely written, let alone spoken, word. Nowadays it ought to be regarded as a 'sponge word' – that is to say, it has become so over-used, even misused, and employed in so many varied ways that its value is questionable, its value being akin to that of 'liberal', which means so many different things to different people. Be that as it may, its original meaning – a happy surprise encounter or occurrence – is how I wish it to be comprehended in the title to the present chapter.

Once standardisation became the ethos of the last few decades, much of the older, quainter, outdated yet attractive things, artefacts, systems and so on became scarce. It was regarded as a stroke of luck when one came cross something that had somehow survived modernisation, avoided obsolescence while retaining its uniqueness and old-world attraction. Wistfulness, nostalgia and all associated psychologia were thereby heightened. Once a thing is threatened with extinction it becomes precious in the eyes of many. Many were, are and always will be the 'expeditions' to have a last look or relish a last experience. With luck the search will be rewarded, nostalgia indulged. But yet, that is not serendipity, although fortuitous stumbling across more than one had set out to seek on the way could so be classified. True serendipity is the sudden, totally unexpected, unsought-for sight, experience, of something cherishable.

Steam-lovers have always been aware of the existence of some never-yet-encountered locomotives or other railway artefacts. They are truly surprised, joyously, when it unexpectedly comes their way, totally unsought, perhaps not having been given any thought for years on end. What to some enthusiasts is commonplace may crop up as a delicious surprise to another, elsewhere.

Let Edward Thompson's mangling of Nigel Gresley's first-ever 'Pacific', *Great Northern*, illustrate my point. Photographs I had seen in plenty, articles either lauding or cursing the rebuild I had read from time to time, but not once did I clap eyes upon the machine despite countless visits to the GNR main line over the years. One day, when I had a little time free from study and sport, I took the train from Durham to Newcastle-upon-Tyne, faithful Ensign Selfix 820 camera in my pocket. All I had sought was an hour or two snapping trains, relaxing awhile in the mind-pervasiveness of the world of steam transport. Settled on a trolley at the southern end of the station I idly watched the arrival of a train from Edinburgh. Its 'A3' ('Triumphant in his glory now, His "Sceptre" ruleth sway' says the hymn, for such was the loco's name) uncoupled and toddled away to Gateshead shed.

Out of the shadowed sidings slunk the replacement 'Pacific', looking just that little bit unusual. With due jubilation I rejoiced to see *Great Northern*! What a large hunk of good fortune had been served up for me! Ignorant of his being shedded at that time at nearby Heaton, I had never entertained the slightest hope that our paths might cross. Now *that* is what must be appositely appellated 'serendipitous' – it was genuinely a delightful, unplanned, unthought-up surprise. To the local steam-lovers it was a common sight, but to me it was a joyous novelty to at last study from close up and to photograph. Eventually, over the next two years, we did meet in cuttings, on embankments and at platforms. The serendipity, of course, was no longer experienceable, yet the memory of that prime encounter ensured that I regarded *Great Northern* with some affection thereafter, ugliness of rebuild notwithstanding.

In this section there will be, for some, no understanding of why I include something that is commonplace to them. It will be there simply because it entered my steam-watching quite unsought-for, therefore arousing feelings of surprise and pleasure.

Above This was the brace of 'R1' 0-6-0 tanks at Folkestone (see page 41) that helped to slightly raise my spirits after customs officers had confiscated my recently acquired Bolex cine camera – massive duties had been demanded, which I could not afford, and many weeks' carriage cleaner's wages went into rescuing that camera from bondage. My joyously anticipated plan to shoot steam movies of the ex-Southern Railway and the ex-GCR in the course of my journey from Folkestone to Leicester was shattered. To the end of steam, only once did I find myself in Southern territory to capture its steam locomotives on cine film – a large regret then, but of no consequence today.

Below Back on the main line I was hoping to see main-line locomotive stock around, but was afforded a unique photographic opportunity in the form of two more 'R1' tank engines. One has a normal cab height and boiler mountings, whereas the other carries the much reduced versions for working the shallow, narrow-bore tunnel on the then recently closed former Canterbury & Whitstable line.

Above News that the last LNWR 'Cauliflower' had been scrapped was false. Much to my delight we came across her as the school club wandered through Crewe North shed, and this photo filled a gap in my LNWR section, quite apart from thrilling me with her presence.

Above right No 58321 and a sister LNWR 'Coal Engine' (silly, obvious name) had been retained as works shunters in Crewe Works. Appearances suggested that both were in decent working order and respectably clean. Surprisingly, neither was no more considered for preservation than the two stored 'Cauliflowers'. Neither Crewe staff, amongst whom were surely some proud ex-LNWR members, nor their superiors at HQ had shown any interest in ever securing examples of LNWR steam power. Only four years earlier than this photo, the 'Precursor' and 'George V' classes had become extinct without a word in their favour. Neither had the last, though rebuilt, 'Claughton' (No 6004) or the 'Prince of Wales' Class and its goods version been shown mercy. The last LNWR steam motor, No 29988, was still around in 1948, the last of all British examples of this format. I was lucky to snap the last 2-4-0T, No 58092, both

on the Cromford & High Peak line and awaiting cutting-up at Crewe. Surely she, so popular with enthusiasts, could have been spared together with one of the extant 2-4-2 tanks. Let's also not forget the 'Oxo tin' 0-4-2T No 47862, still kicking around in 1954. Oh Crewe! How could you so abandon your heritage?

Below A most lucky shot: station pilots seemed to spend a lot of time lurking in carriage sidings, and this last member of the worthy LNWR 0-6-2T 'Coal Tank' Class appeared unexpectedly in the middle roads of Birmingham New Street station. I was on my way elsewhere, not having intended to test the rumour that she was still there; in fact, no thought at all had been given to the possibility. But there she was, drab and filthy, no sunlight daring to peep out at her from the murky sky. Out came the camera and a muttered plea that it might just secure a shot. It almost let me down, for the negative is a dreadfully thin one. It was this sort of frustration that led me to sell my model railway and eventually spending all holidays working on the railways to purchase a superior camera. The next month's *Railway Magazine* noted her withdrawal.

Below January was never a pleasant month for stomping around sheds and yards. The school railway club members were chilled as we crossed from the Derby sheds to the scrap lines. Scarcely could I believe my eyes when I spotted the remains of an ex-Midland Railway, outside-framed Kirtley 0-6-0, still pretty well intact despite having been withdrawn four years earlier, according to our guide. This negative, produced by ultra-basic Kershaw Penguin camera, is of poor standard, but by modern computer techniques has been

rendered acceptable, which means a lot to me since I never had the fortune to shoot such a loco in steam. This was the last but one shot of the day. My final exposure, a hand-held short time exposure of half of a second, was spent on a 4P Compound; when processed, close examination of the negative revealed in the background an as yet still in service Kirtley outside-framed 0-6-0. Research showed her to be No 58110, indeed the very last survivor. Yes, life has its ironies and disharmonies, I thought to myself with no small sentiments of chagrin.

Below One of my (many) just acceptable photos. Sheer chance brought me to Leicester Midland station just in time to see this decrepit last representative of the Midland Railway 3P 4-4-0s. Lighting was dreadful, my camera primitive. The driver saw my dilemma and invited me to jump on to the tracks, to the misty but vaguely sunny side. Even so, a hand-held half-second exposure was needed. Shortly after, the lovely old lady sauntered off southwards with some stock, heading, I think, for Rugby. A poor shot, but nevertheless one of my favourites: that mystic aura of light fog, an unexpected engine, a whiff of nostalgia for the last of the line, the awareness that this was the unrepeatable chance to photograph her, the kindly driver, the diaphanous disappearance into the murky mist of the enchanting engine, all combined to create a harmonious experience. I almost skipped all the way back home!

Waiting at Chester for a connection to Crewe on my return from the successful interview for my first post, my cup of joy brimmed over as, side by side, stood examples of both versions of Caprotti valve gear as tested on the Stanier 'Black Fives'. The light was good and the angles just right, enabling me to secure a set of shots for comparisons, though, of course, I also studied them for several minutes in the flesh, so to speak. I later met them frequently at Chester since they regularly worked the Manchester route.

Above I had heard tales that a rebuilt 'Scot' was running around with perfectly straight smoke deflectors, but not once did a proving photograph appear in the railway magazines I read. Humble pie was what I ate on Rugby platform when, on my way to London, No 46106 took the down, central avoiding line. A pleasant coincidence, in retrospect, for half a decade earlier I had gazed, enraptured, on the pristine GNoSR 'D40' of the same name, *Gordon Highlander* (see page 21). Many years later, the ex-WD 2-10-0 came my way, unexpectedly, its name, however, truncated to *Gordon*, who later achieved fame as a principal character in the Reverend Awdry's children's tales.

Below Fred and I were totally unaware that a double blastpipe and miniature smoke deflectors had been experimentally fitted to one or two 'V2' 2-6-2s. We stared in amazement at the sight of No 60813 as it left Edinburgh for Aberdeen. Only its unusual exhaust sound had drawn our eyes chimneywards to see what was amiss. Never had our cameras swung so swiftly into action to catch the novelty before it was out of range.

Above At first sight this dirty engine was just another 'Austerity' 2-8-0, until its length seemed unusual. Then we saw the wheels and rejoiced to see our first 'Austerity' 2-10-0. Eastfield shed, large though it was, left little space for photography, and we just managed to squeeze in the great length of this wartime machinery.

Below Packing up our camping kit, Fred and I were scarcely on the lookout for trains, for the line was within a few strides. A chime whistle stopped our mixture of packing and snacking, and we were just in time to photograph this beautifully clean BR Standard '5' at the head of 'The Granite City' express. Had we finished packing just that bit earlier we would have been walking along the main road into Stirling right out of sight of the railway and would thus have missed the glorious express.

Above No 61379 was the original bearer of the famed nameplate *Mayflower*, commemorating that high-risk undertaking of the seventeenth-century Pilgrim Fathers to sail to America to enjoy their own particular brand of Christianity, fleeing the current British bigotry and persecution. One of the delights, but a responsible one, for carriage cleaners at Leicester Central was to ride in the front guard's compartment of shunted, just-arrived excursion stock. After withdrawal from the arrival platform and being pushed back into the station on a different track, the leading coach would be close to that adjacent platform's buffer-stops, which were partly hidden from the driver by the bend in the tracks. Thus the cleaner would apply the brake handle to bring the shunted train to a stop with fine accuracy – we never hit the buffers, halting within a couple of feet. In this instance, following established procedure, I had entered the stock at the front end in the arrival platform to walk through to the rear end (soon to become the front), checking that nothing valuable had been forgotten by the excursionists. I was thus in a fine position to take this photo of *Mayflower* through the doorway as she drew out the coaches to reposition them for

us cleaners to set to and clean, while leaving the arrival platform empty for the next returning holiday train. During the manoeuvre I retraced my steps to reach the far-end guard's compartment with ample time to prepare for the braking process.

Below left Serendipity largely depends on being fortuitously in the right place at the right time. It was never more true than on the occasion when I was walking to the sheds at Burton-on-Trent, which footpath meets the former GNR branch from Stafford at Eggerton Junction. A few moments too soon or too late and I would have missed seeing an ex-GNR 'K2' 2-6-0 coming off the branch to join the Midland line to Bristol.

Top What a surprise to meet a class I had believed extinct! This survivor, No 69093, an ex-NER 'N10' Class 0-6-2T, was caught shunting the quayside in Sunderland, cheekily sporting an express passenger train lamp-code.

Middle The school railway club had targeted Leeds at Easter. Imagine my huge delight on discovering the very last representative of the loco stock of the Hull & Barnsley Railway. Swift slaughter of its motive power followed the 1923 formation of the LNER, though the ex-NER powers were largely responsible since, having to all intents and purposes controlled the smaller company, they had decided on some degree of standardisation, which meant NER engine power. So, with a typical Stirling family round-top cab, there stood, dead, 'N13' 0-6-2T No 69113, the handiwork of Matthew Stirling, who, incidentally, was unique, I believe, in being the only example of a single CME being responsible for the locomotive department throughout the entire lifetime of a railway company.

Bottom The oval 'LNER' logo was to be seen on anything from cake-stands to some locomotives from immediate pre-war days onwards. Long after nationalisation the smaller articles could still be seen in use bearing the logo: tea-towels, chairs, plates and so on. It came as a surprise to see that one remained affixed to the bunker of a 'Q1' 0-8-0 tank at Eastfield shed, six years after the LNER had ceased to exist and all its lettering had been removed from cabsides. How this example had survived is a mystery that provokes numerous explanations in the steam lover's imagination.

Above The school railway club visited Oxley, Tyseley and Wolverhampton sheds one January day. Never-ending dullness and bitter winds really spoiled the outing until, right at the very last moment prior to an awful blizzard, we came across 'Dukedog' No 9018 preparing to draw a freight train out of Oxley yards. Great excitement from the older club members was not offset by youngsters who could see nothing worthwhile in that 'scruffy old crate', as some called it. Happily, enough daylight was still hanging around for my primitive, very basic camera to secure a shot. It would be many years afterwards that I clapped eyes on another example, this time at Wrexham in 1960, though sadly it was not in steam, awaiting scrapping.

Above left My train was drawing past Didcot shed, so the camera was expectant of something. It was not let down. The Cleobury Mortimer & Ditton Priors branch served military establishments while passing through well-forested areas, and fire could be utterly disastrous. At the War Department's behest, spark-arresting apparatus was fitted to locomotives working the line. These two Panniers were on shed either for servicing or even for scrap, for the branch was in its final death throes.

Left It seemed too good to be true. Pre-1948-liveried locos were exceedingly rarely encountered by my camera since photography had not been available to me until 1950, by which time most engines had been 're-badged'. This Pannier, steamless at Oswestry, must certainly have been given a repaint for

some special purpose, for the year was 1964 – sixteen years after nationalisation. Even so, it was a delightfully lucky day for me to see such good paintwork. Then, sadly, the pre-'48 illusion was shattered when I walked around the engine – the BR standard-issue smokebox number plate was there for all to see. Ah well!

Above Camped south of Aberystwyth, my breakfast was interrupted by the passage of one of the final trains on the Carmarthen to Aberystwyth line. Fortunately my camera was well within reach. Calling at the station before moving on, I was disappointed not to snap other trains arriving or departing along that cross-country route. Within months the threat of closure, pasted up on the station walls, was implemented and that beautiful line was lost for ever.

Above right The cycling goal one day had been to explore Wells Cathedral. On the outskirts of the city we were halted by closed level crossing gates, and along the Cheddar Valley line came this permanent way train in the charge of a Collett '2251' 0-6-0. Like us, it paused momentarily by the crossing, seeming to crave a photograph. I duly obliged, happy to have secured, so unexpectedly, a record of the lovely branch line. Note the interesting signal.

Right This is serendipity par excellence. Having glutted our cameras with the 'Plant Centenarian' Ivatt 'Atlantics' special and a host of expresses on Stoke Bank, friend Fred and I began our ride home, pausing, as was our wont, on Careby Bridge, next to which stood the local primary school. Our camera activity caught the attention of Mr Barbary, the headmaster. He graciously invited us into his lounge for a pot of tea and biscuits, but his real intention was to give us a wonderful, visual delight. All round the room were superb large-gauge models of steam engines, every one exquisitely constructed by Mr Barbary – and they could all work. His pride and joy was a wonderfully finished, perfect replica of a Great Western 'Saint', No 2908 *Lady of Quality*. Mr Barbary relished the name he had chosen, for to him it typified GWR engineering, while to us it spoke eloquently of

the beautiful quality of his engineering skills. Fixed to the wall over the mantelpiece was a glowing nameplate formerly carried by 'Duke' 4-4-0 No 3274 *Cornishman*. Mr Barbary explained that being himself a Cornubian he had placed an order, well in advance, to secure that nameplate immediately the locomotive was withdrawn. It had cost him £4 plus carriage costs, quite a sum at the time. Permission was sought and readily given for us to photograph the nameplate, of which a copy was promptly despatched to Mr Barbary. Today, what is its value? Astronomical I should think. But where is it, where are his glorious models? Does anyone know? I would love to find out.

Above Braving the snow-threatening weather, I went for a cycle ride through the hills around Llangollen, a round trip of more than 30 miles, but enough in view of the weather. Frozen to the core I descended from the tops after a challenging rough-trackway route to seek a café for that essential pot of tea. Thawed and re-energised, I straddled my beloved Claud Butler cycle and set off again to face the climb up the Horseshoe Pass with its exhilarating swoop down the other side followed by half-a-dozen miles of gentle lane rides back home. Obviously, steam trains were no part of the day's purpose.

Crossing the bridge over the rampaging rain-and-snow-melt-swollen Dee, I was nevertheless seduced by the Lorelei-power song of a steam train. Glancing across to the station naturally slowed the cadence of my pedalling. The lure was too strong. Off the bike, camera out and *Odney Manor*, working one of the final week's Barmouth-Wrexham services, was embedded in photographic emulsion. It was a contenting moment or so for me: everything felt balanced, co-ordinated. A novel, exhilarating cycle excursion, a pleasant rest in a café, a beautifully situated railway station by a powerfully appealing river, and the final chord in all this harmony was the gentle soughing of the safety valve of the 'Manor'. The lively turbulence of the River Dee was orchestrated still further by the sharp, eager exhaust when *Odney* set off on the last stage of his long journey from snow-covered, wild beauty to semi-industrialised Ruabon and Wrexham. I just had to cross the road to watch him churn out his smoke – that nasal nectar – lean to the curve and fade away. Had I not done so, my feelings would have felt similar to those experienced when the radio accidentally gets turned off just as the last few bars of a glorious symphony are raising the mind into the expectancy of a fine resolution of theme and orchestration.

Left En route for Gloucester to celebrate Easter in its superb cathedral, I ceased pedalling awhile at Evesham, for my personal firebox needed a round or two shovelling in it, not of coal but of cheese and Marmite sandwiches. Naturally the station platform was my dining area. Scarcely had the goodies been unwrapped when the 'peg' dropped. Camera seized in the hope of something unusual, I rose and went to the platform edge. Such a disappointment – a mere commonplace 'Hall', and the camera was lowered. But should it have been? Casually glancing at the nameplate, I was delighted to read *Saint Martin*, the very founder-member of the 'Hall' Class,

experimentally a smaller-wheeled rebuild of a 'Saint' Class loco. Interestingly, once the endless string of hall names was under way, no one thought to re-name *Saint Martin* to bring him into line. So, up went the camera just as the blower was put on and the first chuff was on its way to the chimney. The shutter fired to give me a triply valued negative: the 'Saint' that had sired the 'Halls', a record of the GWR station, and the happy recall that my happy singing days were spent in Leicester Cathedral, which was dedicated to St Martin.

Above left I was heading for a short-break walking holiday in Derbyshire, the well-inbuilt hobby of steam-watching accompanying me every mile of the way. One or two trains were photographed but nothing out of the ordinary was noted until, somewhere near Belper, I noticed an old but well-maintained ex-Midland Railway board signal patently still doing its job. This simply must be photographed, thought I, with my camera at the ready – my usual practice when travelling. Other boards I had seen in past years had been grotty, rotted or simply too awkwardly located for a snapshot, which meant that at last I had secured an example in fine condition. How old it was is anyone's guess. Was it periodically renewed, replaced or what?

Above Driving through new territory, somewhere near Dunlop, after a climbing holiday in Scotland, I was halted all of a sudden by the sight of an array of signals set at Danger, the reason for which was immediately apparent. Twenty yards or so further on, the road bridge had been removed, leaving a nasty sheer drop for any train to fall over. I looked at the scene more with amusement than out of railway interest.

Below During one of my infrequent steam 'fixes' on Durham station this rare train, hauled by four-times lucky 'L1' 2-6-4T – No 67777 – hove into sight. Always suspicious what a one-coach train might be, my camera was out and ready, two shots being taken of the CMME special. With hindsight, I ought to have taken a broadside shot of the coach, for who knows what dignitary or top engineering boffin might have been on board. Already travelling fast, the 'L1' accelerated through the station and charged across the viaduct, wagging its stubby little tail behind him, doubtless to the consternation and discomfort of those within. The reason for the excess alacrity was very shortly explained by the descent of the 'Queen of Scots' Pullman hot on his tail, seemingly going faster than the 'L1'.

Above En route to Euston, my head, as usual, out of the window, near Hemel Hempstead I noticed a short train ahead on the slow line. It included an ancient-looking coach. Out came my Selfix camera and was swiftly readied for action. 2P 4-4-0 No 40672 had been well cleaned up for her important task of pulling an engineers' inspection train. But surely something else catches the eye? Just look at that gorgeous old coach!

Below In the distance near Borth, a strangely headboarded engine was observed trailing an unusual-looking coach. With ample time to spare, my breath was regained after a strenuous cycle ride to permit a shake-free shot of whatever this odd assemblage might be. It proved to be an inspectors' train, though what they were inspecting I could not find out. There was a lot of moving about in the coach when it stopped, but no one descended. Two snaps were taken before the special shot off northwards and I approached the station porter. He, too, was none the wiser, merely commenting, 'The high-ups are always nosing around for something.'

7
NARROW GAUGE

I was in two minds about presenting this section. A visit to any of the deliciously enchanting narrow-gauge lines' shops will present the enthusiast with beautifully crafted photographic publications and postcards, all of the society's own production. Happily, sales boom, assisting to fund the upkeep of the society's treasures.

For years now there has been this wealth of dedicated publications of the highest standards, by amateurs and professionals. So why should I bother, being nowhere near such perfection and lacking their total coverage of every aspect of the narrow-gauge scene, 'said to myself, said I' (courtesy of Messrs Gilbert & Sullivan)?

The thought that my photographs, taken in the pre-modern-colour-film era, might make a change for some enthusiasts encouraged me to sort out my few negatives. Why few? Because I bought the societies' superior products!

Additionally, the very title of this book, *Steam: The Mystic Harmony*, decided that I include a narrow-gauge section because surely no one can

The earliest of rescued railways, the Talyllyn inspired not only the preservation movement for narrow-gauge systems but also gave considerable encouragement to those enthusiasts somewhat hesitant about standard-gauge preservation. We are greatly indebted to Messrs Rolt and company for kick-starting what has become an enthralling variety of lines and locomotives across Britain. Here a smoky start is made out of Towyn (Tywyn) as the severe gradient is tackled by *Edward Thomas* (great-grandfather of my wife, incidentally, assuming the engine is named after the famed Welsh poet and not some local dignitary).

dispute that a session on a narrow-gauge line does engender an other-worldly, mystic awareness with its unsought aura of harmony. It is just there, without the need to seek or hope for it. Whether on board the train or comfortably settled with a tea-flask, a pair of scrumptious 'Sam Widges', portable chair and camera equipment somewhere up the line, the air of the expectancy of being taken away into a beyond-current-times dimension envelops the enthusiast, the entire railway environment girt about, even into the distance, by ineffably glorious scenery. So many locations along the line are so devoid of modern habitations, of car-choked roads, that the approaching train is unwittingly viewed as being actually in the mid-to-late-nineteenth century, that period during which we all would have loved to have lived (though only because of the ubiquity of the steam railway, of course).

We feel, strangely, a mixture of excitement and relaxation in this wide-awake dream experience. We have a peculiar feeling of being in concord with ourselves and with what we are indulging in:

the train approaches, passes; we watch, we listen, we inhale; we might fire our cameras, all the while exclaiming aloud our nigh worship along with our companions, or perhaps quietly within ourselves, releasing our crowding sentiments. Then, all is past, echoes fade, smoke dissipates. We are returned, sanely, to our habitual, diurnal selves, but even so recognising that 'we have been somewhere', in some beautiful harmonious experience.

Peculiarly, this experience seems less quintessentially available in the standard-gauge environment, even where it is magnificently possible to run preserved locomotives with totally appropriate stock within a fully nineteenth-or-mid-twentieth-century environment inclusive of signal boxes, signals and telegraph poles hung with humming wires. Why this lessening of the experience? I cannot say other than that the narrow gauge, its miniatureness notwithstanding, exerts a mystic power through which we sense more strongly our one-ness with the steam railway, something beyond our admiration and respect.

Now purely devoted to the tourist industry, all narrow-gauge railways' original, industrial purposes are all but forgotten. As a reminder, this photo depicts the Welshpool & Llanfair Light Railway engaged in its original activity. Nameplate-less

ex-GWR No 823 *Countess* storms comfortably through sylvan beauty on her way to Llanfair with a train of fully loaded coal wagons.

Above Historically interesting, at Porthmadoc one of the Ffestiniog Railway company's locomotives is seen taking on water but also coal in the days before conversion to oil-burning. Since that conversion the exhaust no longer recalls the mildly mentally intoxicating breath of good old burning king coal, but nor does it blast forth cinders to sting our eyes and set the lineside forests ablaze.

Below Of all the many narrow-gauge railways, the Snowdon Mountain Railway was the only one conceived and built entirely to cash in on the tourist industry in North Wales. Walkers in the springtime can learn whether or not the summit of Snowdon is snowbound by observing whether or not the day's trains are running. Catering and auxiliary staff for the summit café/restaurant are taken up by train. Thus, heavy snow means no trains, means no staff, means no chance of refreshment at the top, means carry up you own food (which any sensible walker would do, anyway, café notwithstanding). This view, taken when I was walking the full Snowdon Horseshoe circuit, shows an upward train within a few hundred yards of the summit station.

8
ON SHED

Irresistible, that's what locomotive sheds were to each and every steam-lover! Akin to bees buzzing around the hive, sometimes going in, sometimes setting off for distant places, similar steam engine activity around a shed exerted a powerful attraction, perhaps greater in some ways than that which we experienced as we sat by the lineside watching them pass before us.

Was it the concentrated power of so many in one location that inspired our awe? Was it a more mundane urge, the chance to 'cop' a large number all in one go? Certainly any visit to a previously unknown depot would present numerous fine pickings to the number-bagger, and probably to the photographer as well. Could it be that curiosity about what went into the preparing of a locomotive for its day's work drew us there, or the manner in which it was disposed of when its business with coach or wagon was over? Was there perhaps some strange voyeuristic impulse that incited us to go and spy on the engines in their private boudoir where they were not really watchfully on their guard, so to speak, for there was always a guilty feeling of sorts when we 'bunked' a shed – not necessarily out of the fear of getting nabbed by the railway police? Was it our desire to show off before our peers, to display bravado, that challenged us to enter the portals of a forbidden realm, that lay behind our aim to sneak up to 'burgle' this engine sanctuary, to 'steal' names and numbers in order to swell our 'swag-bag' stock books? Well, which of you knows the answer?

Maturer and respectful of the law, combined with the desire to be able to wander and study without fear, led us to apply for shed permits. Yet the thrill of the chase was diminished by not one jot nor tittle. Excitement, anticipation, anxieties remained as powerful as in the days of our brash, early teens. Number-bagging had been superseded by wiser attitudes towards the steam engine. We wanted to peer between the frames of a static locomotive to mentally wrestle with its inside valve gear components, to work out what went where, to see the linkages of the brake system… We wanted to be able to contemplate the full outlines and format of an engine with none of it hidden by station platforms, with ampler time than that which a temporary halt at a station allowed us. We have chatted with footplate staff in stations often enough, but in the sheds we could pass the time of day with fitters and, above all, with shed superintendents, gleaning scraps of fresh knowledge. The list is probably endless, for each enthusiast seeks his own particular satisfaction during the time spent in and around the loco sheds.

Whatever the motivation, our moments or hours spent shed-bashing were always happy, rewarding and exciting.

Above right Arriving at Leicester Belgrave Road (GNR) station to begin my annual summertide slog as cleaner, etc, I was stopped dead in my tracks, for there in a bay stood former, hated rival Midland Railway engines, the preserved 'Spinner' and the 2-4-0. Permission to sprint home and collect a camera was given in return for a promise to work through my lunch hour. Shots were duly taken. In the course of the afternoon we took our 30-minute tea-break, during which time a 'J6' removed the locos. Camera still to hand, I sprinted along two platforms, leapt across three tracks and took a picture of the trio. The 'J6' then shunted them into the near-derelict GNR shed. Our later, final, tea-break saw me foregoing my much-needed cuppa – I was busy in the loco shed, shooting the two locos. Later the fitters removed axle-box parts, etc, to safeguard them during the return journey to their storage homes; the side rods of the 2-4-0 were later removed for the same reason.

Right We should have felt honoured by the daily presence of the *Flying Scotsman* on the ex-GC line through Leicester. Perhaps initially we were, but after a few reports that it did not perform too well, and never being properly – if at all – cleaned, looking a general scruff, novelty and pride soon wore off. He was often seen running tender-first on locals – quite a come-down. Here he is on Leicester shed on one of the cleaner days, ash and clinker strewn in piles at his side.

Opposite page Excitement always preceded our cycling trips to Leicester Great Central sheds, for one never knew what to expect. Before my camera days, many rarities had been seen, such as GCR named 4-6-0s, or a 'D9'. Even after these had gone the way of all rusty corpses, surprises would come our way, alongside the diurnally expected. These pictures provide a portrait of a particularly surprising afternoon visit. Bikes propped up against the railings separating shed from canal towpath, we spied something beneath the sheer-legs, so over the railings we went to discover an original Raven 'B16' about to be hoisted up for some under-belly examination and repair (*far left*). 'B16s' were regular performers on what we called 'The York Goods', a fast goods that passed northwards late in the evening after pausing for water in the loop lines of Leicester Goods South, but to meet one (No 61450) in distress on shed was novel. Note the pile of fire-bricks in the foreground.

Equally unexpected was a Thompson 'L1' 2-6-4T, No 67762, likewise parked by a stack of fire-bricks (*below left*). They were infrequent visitors to the line, usually working Nottingham-Leicester locals. Shortly afterwards she was hauled clear by a 'J52' and drawn into the shed.

Some time later out of the shed came 'B1' No 61316 (*above near left*), smokebox adorned with 'The Master Cutler' headboard, the armorial shields nicely polished up. Not one of our engines, being a Sheffield lassie, she would obviously return home that evening after taking over from whatever brought 'The Cutler' as far as Leicester.

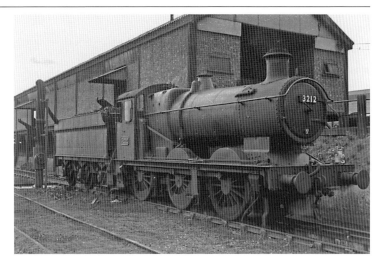

This page Likewise, in the south, Eastleigh offered me great delights in great variety. First I met Collett 0-6-0 No 3212 coaling up after travelling the Didcot, Newbury & Southampton line (*top*). A bevy of pre-1923 engines stood outside the main shed, including a brace of LB&SCR 'E4' 0-6-2Ts, an 'M7' and a 'T9' of LSWR parentage (*middle*). Walking further afield I stumbled across an early acquaintance – *Bude* (*bottom*)– first seen working the Great Central line during the 1948 loco exchanges. She looked the worse for wear, and due for major overhaul, I suspected.

Above Ryde shed welcomed spotters. I spent a happy half-hour just idling around and looking, raising the camera less than half a dozen times, for there was next to no choice in motive power. A couple of 'O2' 0-4-4 tanks were ready for off, Nos 34 *Newport* and 28 *Ashey*. Behind them lurked 'AIX' 0-6-0T *Freshwater*, bearing number 8.

Below Bournemouth shed is best seen from the train, I thought, as we steamed through on the way to Weymouth Harbour. On shed was a rebuilt Bulleid 'Pacific', flanked by two BR Standards, a 2-6-4T and Class 5 No 73029.

Right On shed at Hasland, cheek by jowl stand two contrasting versions of Midland Railway 0-4-0 tanks. In the background stands No 41518 with Salter spring balance safety valves, saddle-cum-pannier tanks and inside cylinders. Contrasting with her we have No 41531 with updated safety valves, full-sized side tanks and outside cylinders and valve gear.

Right Our gang of young spotters didn't think much of this gawky-looking engine, unappreciative of what fine machines these Lancashire & Yorkshire Railway 2-4-2 fast passenger tanks were. Our sample, No 50887, is standing in wan sunlight – ideal for photography – outside Newton Heath shed, the major depot of the L&YR.

Below One week after I took ownership of my first camera, the school railway club paid visits to Toton and Derby sheds. A dreadful snowstorm savaged us as we staggered and slithered our way to Toton. The snow-bedecked line of Garratts and 0-6-0s suggested an interesting photograph and, given the primitive specification of my camera, I was surprised that it yielded a passably attractive print.

Above A favoured haunt of spotters was Swain Street walkway, which stretched almost the full length of the LMS loco sheds from the end of Leicester station, just the other side of the road bridge. This walkway was perched high up and therefore gave a magnificent panoramic view of all passing trains, of all shunting movements and of every shed activity. These advantages can be appreciated from this picture, which also illustrates the pending fates of a line of stored MR locos. The LNWR 'Super D' still works healthily as a BR Standard creeps on to shed and a Class 5 takes on coal.

Below Rotten weather – what can you expect in January? – made for a miserable railway club trip to Tyseley, but once there spirits rose and cameras were pulled out of pockets and cases. We soon did the outside rounds, mainly unexciting beasts of burden, then made our way inside where a few braziers attracted our frozen paws – upper and lower ones. Nothing of novelty value was espied until we came cross an ex-Great Central First World War veteran, 'ROD' 2-8-0 No 3016, one of a batch of around forty purchased from the Government at a knock-down price. She had been 'Great Westernised' with regard to her boiler mountings but otherwise remained in original condition. The GWR operating department thought highly of these engines, retaining them well into nationalisation years, which was a better fate than that meted out to the score or so bought by the LNWR, which wanted them merely to counter a desperate shortage of tenders; these were retained for years whereas the locos went extremely early to the scrap heap and the melting pot.

Above It was 1950, and I was wildly excited by my first camera, even though it was very basic indeed. Cycling far away from local steam haunts, I hoped to bag something different, perhaps historic. Shrewsbury shed, for a young lad, supplied some such wants: a 'Saint' and two 'Stars'. One of the latter was parked too close to the fence, but the other, No 4015, stood in ample space. Standing on the crossbar of my bike to reach over the high fence, I carefully composed my first respectable shot of a famous class – *Knight of St John.*

Below The following four photographs typify what Chester shed was like in the early 1960s. The first portrays a dead 2P 4-4-0 with an attendant 'Jinty' 0-6-0.

Left Further general views of Chester shed, with a 'Royal Scot', Class 5s of LMS or BR make, various versions of 2-6-4 tanks, pre-and-post-1948 designs, 'Moguls' of various designs and the occasional sample of ex-GWR stock, though the latter merely called for coal and water, never being allocated to the shed.

Right After a tough cycle ride from Mold, Machynlleth was reached late in the afternoon. Friendly staff more or less encouraged enthusiasts to wander in their shed and around the yard – goods yard excluded. Inside the depot BR light 2-6-0 No 78006 enjoys its weekly boiler wash-out.

Right Dull was the day, out was the hope of photography inside Oswestry shed. However, there was no shortage of subject matter outside. After minor repairs this Ivatt 2-6-0 backed out. A couple of fitters faffed around the valve gear for a while, pronounced all was well then left the footplate crew to make for the station. Forty minutes later, sitting on a trolley in the station, I watched her set off with a train for Welshpool.

Below Croes Newydd was not a large shed, hence the regular sight of a line of locos awaiting their turn to go inside for maintenance, some of which, however, was carried out even in poor weather in the open air.

Above While outside Aberdare shed engines were lining up for the scaffold of dismemberment, a few lucky locos could be found in steam inside or out on the line. Here, a brace of magnificent but dirty eight-coupled heavy freight tank engines simmer down after night-hauling coal trains. They both set forth again late that afternoon, one setting off light engine towards Neath, probably to gather wagon-loads from the still numerous colliery sidings. The other sat in the shed yard for half an hour before moving across to the coaling stage and then to the water crane.

Below Elsewhere inside Aberdare shed the driver and fireman of their Pannier tank heave and swivel her on the turntable to line her up with some particular stabling point. Fortunately the huge eight-coupled tank in the background was not theirs to turn, for that would have required huge efforts.

Above A brief sojourn in Aberystwyth just had to include a call at the station to see the narrow-gauge Vale of Rheidol Railway. Waiting for a sight of one of its 2-6-2 tanks, I turned my attention to the standard-gauge shed. No GWR stock was in residence, the sole occupants being this pair of the magnificently efficient BR Standard 2-6-4 engines.

Below While I was resident in the North East, the 'G5s' soon won a place in my affections, for in addition to their well-proportioned format they were stalwart workers throughout the ex-NER system. Many times I travelled behind them, delighting in their clear, throaty exhaust, and smart acceleration and time-keeping. I regarded them as friends, in so far as one can associate pleasant experiences with an inanimate machine. Two 'G5s' are taking their deserved relaxation at Sunderland shed.

Above There was a fair number of 'A1' 'Pacifics' around on the Saturday when I made a half-day pilgrimage to Gateshead. Fed and watered, one such engine ambles off shed to make for the station to take over a southbound train. Unusually there is no sign of the always lengthy queue for the coaling stage – everything must have been out on the line.

Below Ex-NER No 62384 was in splendid order, albeit just a little dusty, as she stood outside Neville Hill shed. I was overjoyed go photograph her, for her class, the 'D20s', had been eluding me for years.

Above Grantham always proved to be one of the most difficult sheds to bunk. However, there was a spot sufficiently close by to permit observation of most shed activities and of what passed by on the main line. Since it was generally crowded by hordes of spotters and a few camera-toters, a railway policeman or other official would come along and make his presence felt, though in a pleasant way. Here 'A4' *Dominion of New Zealand* has just completed the turn-around procedures, and will shortly move off to the station to take over a southbound train.

Below A line-up of freight engines, mainly 2-8-0s, stands ready at Grantham to go to the High Dyke sidings, or to receive of the attention of the fitters, or merely to enter the sheds for the night.

Above To Scotland now, and Edinburgh's Haymarket shed. Quaint Rowland-Emmett-looking, dumb-oak-buffered 'J88' NBR Dock Tank 0-6-0 No 68328 shares cramped parking space with a 'V2' and a 'V3' 2-6-2T.

Below Two generations of express 4-4-0 designs on show at Haymarket shed: a 'Scottish Director', No 62677 *Edie Ochiltree*, and a 'Shire', No 62705 *Lanarkshire*. Both built in the 1920s, they illustrate how much innovation can take place in a very short time.

Right We had not expected to see ex-LNER stock on shed at Edinburgh's LMS Dalry Road shed. Ex-NBR 'N15' 0-6-2 tank No 69187, out of steam, was hemmed in by likewise dead Caledonian 0-4-4 tanks, so could not have escaped to Haymarket anyway.

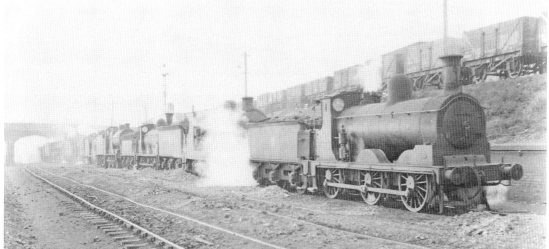

Above Never before or since have I come across such a massive line-up of locomotives eager for coal and water. This mixed bag of ex-Caledonian Railway and LMS motive power greeted Fred and me when we descended to visit St Rollox shed, Glasgow. It was pleasant to have plenty of space within which to photograph most engines independently.

Left One of the few, hence rare, named Stanier Class 5s, No 45156 *Ayrshire Yeomanry*, undergoing serious repair work inside St Rollox shed.

Above On shed at Polmadie, 'Princess Royal' Class 'Pacific' No 46209 *Princess Beatrice* has been serviced ready for her next trip with 'The Mid-day Scot'.

Below This Mackintosh 0-4-4 tank in Forfar shed was permanently fitted with the snowplough, so obviously lay idle for much of the year, which explains why there was no totem on its tank sides. Since its paint-over from LMS lettering to 'British Railways' it had not had to revisit St Rollox for overhaul, given its low annual mileage, so the early nationalised ownership wording remained to be photographed six years on.

Below right His tender removed, a Caledonian 'Jumbo' 0-6-0 reveals his footplate controls inside Stirling shed.

Above Perth MPD was a very busy shed indeed. As we approached it, engines were coming and going all the time. This quick, overall view – we were in a hurry to get inside out of the rain – was taken in an attempt to capture the activity.

Below In 1954 Stanier 'Black Fives' had not yet snaffled all workings on the West Highland Line. In this general view of Fort William shed one such class member can be seen, but in the company of a 'K4', a 'B1' and some NBR 'J36s'.

Left Steamless, ex-Great North of Scotland Railway 'D40' 4-4-0 No 62279 *Glen Grant* sits quietly in Kittybrewster shed. Note the stack of essential fire-bricks to the right – were they destined for nearby 'K2' No 61792?

Above The number of this 'D40' was indecipherable beneath a thick overcoat of grime, and the neighbouring 'K2' and Class 5 locos were in scarcely better condition as they off-loaded ash outside Kittybrewster. Even pouring rain was incapable of giving the tarnished trio a cleansing scrub-down.

Left How fortunate that examples of both 'Z4' and 'Z5' 0-4-2 dock tanks stood in line for the camera in Kittybrewster shed. Neither was in steam, an ominous sign.

Above Drafted in from their home grounds of Eastern England, the small-boilered 'B12/1' ex-Great Eastern Railway 4-6-0s had been chosen to assist in the hauling of the much heavier trains – due to the importation of bigger, stolid Gresley coaches – along the GNoSR lines. Pal Fred and I had managed a quick from-the-window shot of No 61539 at Cairnie Junction, and assumed that was the last we would see of her. An hour or so later, emerging from a delicious exploration of Keith shed, we were flabbergasted to see that she had tailed us, standing ready positioned for further photographs out in the yard. We had used up three more negatives each before this lovely engine eased her way back to the station to take up once more her duties with a five-strong Gresley-coached train, which, alas, was too distant for us to photograph.

Below Ex-GNoSR 'D40' No 62265 is only just 'on shed', for she was on her way out of Elgin shed to pick up her coaches for services emanating from there.

9
DEATH ROW

'Thy beauty, long desired
Hath vanished from our sight.
Thy power is all expired
And quenched the light of light.'
Paul Gerhardt & Robert T. Bridges,
from 14th-century Latin.

So might we have sung a dismal dirge when faced with a withdrawn or partially scrapped locomotive, forlorn in its battered and rusting condition. We recalled the cheering whistle, the roar of the exhaust from seemingly joyful performances in the days of yore when our hymn might well have been utterly different:

'Oh praise ye the Lord!
All things that give sound
Each jubilant chord re-echo around.'

A certain degree of perverseness emerged from the soul of the steam lover as he went off to haunt scrap yards:

'These are they whose hearts were riven
Sore with woe and anguish tried.'

but yet who derived much pleasure from the contemplation of the destruction wrought upon their formerly favoured locomotive. But then isn't human nature like that in other matters? There are those who smugly show contentment when news meets them that misfortune, nay even death, has visited an acquaintance. An elder lady once advised me: 'Never relate your misfortunes and losses to anyone. Half of those you tell couldn't care less, whilst the other half are happy about it.'

Happily for most of us, visits to a locomotive graveyard were occasioned by a sense of respect, intensified for some into an anthropomorphic assumption that we could share in the sadness of the engines themselves – which of course is a

foolish state of mind to be discouraged at all costs. The only satisfaction derived from the visit for many of us was to have met – at last! – a famed locomotive that had eluded us all those years.

Personally speaking, I derived pleasure from encountering ex-Great Eastern Railway 2-4-0s in Cambridge yard, even though their destiny was to be hacked up. Being a type that I had longed to see, a historic format that had served our early railways so well, I was at last permitted to behold a few in the flesh, moribund though they were. All that I had read about them took on life and meaning beyond mere knowledge. What is the difference between my wish to clap eyes on 'the real E4' and that of the armchair anthropologist who eventually gets to gaze upon a 'real mummy'? He is no longer dependent on other people's photographs in books. Perhaps he can experience the same feelings as he stares at the ancient corpse as did the archaeologist who had unearthed it. I could not picture a live 'E4' much more readily. Most delightfully, half an hour later an active member of the class emerged from Cambridge shed to confirm my musings, but even had she not done so the doornail-dead example nevertheless would have been sufficient.

'A Great and Might Wonder', Gresley's 72,940lb tractive effort Garratt 2-8-8-2T, spent her life far, far away from my home, way beyond my day's cycling range of miles and energy. Photographs of her fighting up Worsborough Incline and later undergoing trials on the Lickey Incline gave some indication of massive proportions and power output. While I was scouring Gorton's graveyard and 'dissection' acreage she gently eased in to stand at the end of the line-up of condemned. The brown-raincoated official descended from the footplate to suggest we have a good look at her, for once steam had dissipated and the fire dead, the 'U1' would never again turn a wheel with her own energy. Disappointed that such magnificence should be cut up, melted down and converted into overbridges along new motorways, I scanned her with respect and some sort of grief. She was photographed only after I was sure that her appearance was embedded firmly in my memory cells. Had No 69999 not been destined for 'death', I could never have seen her, relished her, in order to store up worthy memories of her magnificence.

Only when a steam locomotive is dead and being cut up do we get the salutary jolt that puts all locomotives into emotional perspective: they are nothing more than pieces of metal, carefully, scientifically joined up in such a way as to be of service to mankind. They have no soul, no vibrant personality other than those that we append to them on account of their seeming life, 'revealed' to us by noise, sight and smell. We enjoyed the self-deception just as we can deceive ourselves into believing that rays of coloured lights projected on to the silver screen are living, three-dimensional verities.

Thus, Death Row fills in gaps in our knowledge, brings about mildly sad nostalgia, but, above all, is powerfully salutary!

For years I had longed to see some old, attractive Great Eastern Railway locomotives, and the school club outing promised some degree of fulfilment. Descending at Cambridge after a long cross-country journey, no ancient crockery was in sight, so hopes were pinned on the sheds. Only an hour later did I have the satisfaction of snapping a living 'E4' 2-4-0 as it crept out of the shed. Before that I had had to content myself with shots of dead-as-a-doornail old-timers. A line of wretched 2-4-0s and their 2-4-2 tank versions was saddening after all I had read about them and studied in picture form. No 67221 was a member of the small class of twenty 'F6s'. No 62780, an 'E4' 2-4-0 despite some rust, looked fit to go out on the line with her sister, No 62790, parked behind her.

Above   On seeing this forlorn acreage of condemned locomotives at Severn Tunnel Junction, words from Lewis Carroll's poem 'The Walrus and The Carpenter' came to mind: 'I weep for you, the walrus said, I deeply sympathise ... holding a pocket handkerchief before his streaming eyes.' I certainly did not weep copious tears, but experienced a sharp pang of sorrow at the sight of what were patently still highly serviceable steam engines. This was my very first encounter with such wanton destruction. Scrap lines of worn-out engines I had seen many times and accepted their fate as justifiable in the interest of railway economy and progress, but this untoward destruction I found hard to swallow.

Left   No 58193 stands with several fellow 2Fs on the dead-line in Wellingborough yard. Some looked quite serviceable so, hopefully, may well have been stored for possible future emergencies.

Left   There was surely no hope of a reprieve for this dreadfully woebegone 'Tilbury Tank'. No 41966 had literally been put out to grass at Wellingborough, for she was dumped at the end of a remote, overgrown siding that I stumbled across purely by accident.

Above Ex-LTSR 3P 4-4-2T No 41938 awaits its fate, all alone amidst the buffers and bits of previous executions in Derby scrap yard.

Right There was nothing left of some executed ex-Midland Railway locomotives beyond this stack of old round-top-boiler mountings in Derby's scrap heaps. What would a collector pay today for some of them?

Right Unaware that I would see such original Midland Railway mountings still alive and well on a 1F tank at Rotherham years later, I knew I ought to grab a shot of those on a condemned 2F 0-6-0 at Derby.

Left 'What a dreadful photograph!' you may well exclaim. I agree, but this engine just had to be taken in dreadfully dark weather in a poky storage line outside Derby Works. Photographed in January 1950, this former North London Railway 0-4-2 crane saddle tank was all of ninety-two years old. Never having received a BR renumber, No 27217 was under consideration for preservation at the time. Wary of such plans never being carried through (memories of ex-LNWR express engines of a few years earlier, mooted for preservation but callously cut up), I hand-held a one-second exposure – better a poor photo than no record at all. Needless to say, No 27217 was slaughtered for scrap not long afterwards. Elsewhere similar hopes were booted out in the case of any of the three (ten years younger) ex-GER 'J92' 0-6-0 crane tanks Nos 68867/68/69.

Left After a year abroad I returned to see that entire locomotive classes had been scrapped or stored ready for reprocessing. Grieving at the absence of my much-loved ex-NER 0-4-4Ts and 4-6-2Ts, I hunted down what remained. No 'G5s' were found, but in Sunderland yard two whole lines of 'Pacific' tanks stood stock still for my camera – no steam, no wheels turning, every indication of their moribund condition. Two months later they had gone, hauled off to Darlington for the final rites.

Opposite bottom A sorry sight to greeted at Aberdare as I sneaked along after finding a hole in the fence was this line of stored or for-scrap ex-GWR locos. The nearer Churchward 2-8-0 and a Pannier tank looked quite work-worthy on closer inspection. Most locos had had their brass numberplates removed – light-fingered enthusiasts had to be thwarted. Later the same year (1963) the line-up had increased twofold, while signs of serious rusting had begun to mar the earlier parked engines.

Right No 62659 *Worsley-Taylor* was the last-built and last to go to scrap of the original GCR 'Director' 'D10' Class 4-4-0s of 1913. After a busy life-span of forty years, here he lies, bereft of all personality beyond his cabside number in Gorton scrapyard.

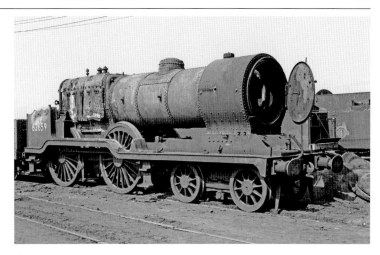

Right Also at Gorton the 'Q1' has its final rest from shunting among many condemned locos waiting alongside.

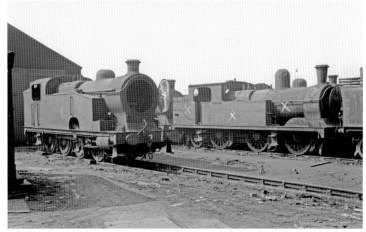

Below Built in 1910, Caledonian Railway 3P 4-4-0 No 54452 stands withdrawn and forlorn at the head of other ex-Caledonian engines, a pair of 0-4-4 tank engines and, surprisingly, a 'Jumbo' in the dead sidings at Inverness in 1954.

Above Although their chimneys were 'pudding-bagged', suggesting temporary storage, it was very unlikely that ex-Caledonian Railway 4-4-0 No 54483 and her sister would steam again. They sat forlornly in the dead sidings at Inverness watching their usurpers, the Stanier Class 5s, comfortably undertaking all their work.

Below It was a surprise to see a late-built Reid 0-6-0 suffering the ignominy of premature scrapping in the outer yards of the GNoSR Inverurie Works in 1954. In the background a 'D11' partners it in their death throes.

Above After relishing the splendid turn-out of *Gordon Highlander* inside Inverurie Works (see page 21), Fred and I strolled around the 'mortuary' area outside. Various engines were in process of dismemberment, a Scottish 'Director' and a couple of 0-6-0s, while dumped further afield almost forgotten half-way through the quartering process stood two seriously truncated, unclassifiable hulks. However, in between them stood what was patently the cadaver of a 4-4-0. A very short distance away, to one side, stood its cab, one of the non-side-window type, proving the engine to be the last of the 1893 'D41' Class. No number was visible anywhere, so your guess as to its identity is as good as was ours at the time.

Below The Scottish 'Director' in the early stages of scrapping at Inverurie, its various parts being added to the scrap pile in the foreground.

Above Wonderfully illustrated books have been published by experts in the art of recording the funereal ambience of Dai Woodham's famous South Wales scrapyard. Having relatives in Barry, a personal visit to the death rows was planned and a half-day consecrated to contemplating line upon line of locos in limbo. This is the grievous sight that greeted me.

Below If you regard Barry scrapyard as unique, think again! Touring around eastern France with a French colleague we came across an astonishing vista of several long lines of defunct steam engines. I could not believe my eyes, even though I had been aware for a long time of the change-over to electric traction in France. It was dusk, the district quite remote. After a very hot day had caused expansion of the iron and steel, cool evening brought about its contraction. Eerie cracks, mild slithering noises and even hisses as slightly heated compressed air was squeezed out of poor joints enveloped us with a ghostly ethos for a few minutes. Fading light made photography an urgent duty so, walking alongside and clambering aboard this vast jail of condemned motive power, I hastily grabbed a record of something that I believed I would never again have to contemplate throughout my remaining years. That was in 1956, when steam ruled with scarcely a challenge, yet it was a mere decade away from similar scenes across Great Britain.

10
A BIT OF COLOUR

'All things bright and beautiful…'

The very little use of colour film for my railway photography is explained by three fundamental factors. During my earliest years of interest in railways, with few exceptions we saw scruffy, war-worn, overworked locomotives. Drabness was but rarely relieved by glorious colour, black, white, grey and filth ruling the rails. Second, our photographing heroes in steam publications used nothing but monochrome to capture the glories of trains and locomotives. We mere beginners ached to achieve their high standards and so locked our minds and film stocks into monochrome portrayals. Articles such as 'Twenty-five Years of Railway Photography' in *The Railway Magazine* were avidly, enviously studied, all their advice taken to heart with the supporting, inspirational black and white masterpieces. The third factor is due to the fascination of the steam train itself. Although livery – if clean – was appreciated, the soul-

Returning from our honeymoon in Ireland, via Fishguard, our 'Manor'-hauled train was held up for quite some time at Llandeilo, allowing me to abandon my wife to nip along the adjacent platform to discover the cause of delay. A mucky 0-6-0PT, hitched to a couple of coaches after taking on water, was awaiting the road to clear after the imminent departure of a freight train from the sidings behind a '43XX' Churchward 'Mogul'. The Clayton diesel like as not had its rôle, too, in the hold-up.

grabbing sounds and movements were the paramount attractions. Did we really care deeply about the spotless condition of No 6220 *Coronation* hurtling through Brinklow, or did we relish far more the sight and sounds of her roaring exhaust, clattering wheels, the blur of valve motion, the lateral sway as she leaned to the curve? All we considered, photographically, was to attempt to capture the ethos of violent movement and thunderous racket.

Even when presented with a fresh-from-work liveried engine, thoughts about recording the colour never entered our minds. Certainly we committed the glory to our memories, which were readily conjured up in full when the monochrome portrait was studied in later years. So far as cine film was concerned, monochrome was more frequently employed, but when this was withdrawn from the market, Kodachrome 25 ASA became the sole film stock, consequently obliging my movie collection to become largely a colour one. Even the sight of GWR 'Kings' flashing across the screen in shining Brunswick green, or sparkling 'A4s' racing down Stoke Bank, failed to enthuse me into colour prints or slides. What few print or slide colour films were used came into my hands more or less fortuitously: very cheap end-of-line offers and two received as presents. Given the very limited exposure latitude for colour, the risk of failure seemed great – just half a stop too much or too little and the photo was irreparably of a poor standard. Chester, Durham, Newcastle and Grantham are the sparse locations where only just acceptable shots were taken.

Time, too, has taken its degrading toll. Modern colour film stock seems unaffected by age, while being tolerant of inaccurate exposure, so I unfailingly employ it on my occasional safari to a steam centre, though monochrome still comes along for the ride, providing a little exercise for roll-film cameras. No preservation period photos are included here since the real experts, wielding high-quality equipment, have already published vast quantities of superb 'stuffed steam' albums.

Well before reaching Grantham, all down non-stop expresses emitted a lengthy warning shriek, setting the anticipation tingles wildly up our spines. The dulcet tones of the station announcer advising passengers to stand well clear of the platform edge would keep up this anticipation still more. It recalled the bidding prayer in a cathedral preceding the beauties of a stately-robed choir and clergy procession before the elevating resonances of the organ envelope all in the mystique of choral matins or evensong. The blurred nature of this shot testifies to the terrific speed of this Peppercorn masterpiece, 'A1' No 60149 *Amadis*.

Above At a more leisurely pace, 2-8-0s of all ex-LNER classes fought their way to and from the High Dyke branch a short way north of Stoke Tunnel, moving vast tonnages of iron ore in the days when we still had a decent steel industry. From the far east-side platform, a gaggle of these hard-worked engines could be seen taking a breather or coming off shed at most times of the day. Frequently with them stood the breakdown train, crane, mess and tool vans with a 'B12' 4-6-0 at their head; when this shot was taken of a High Dyke tripper, this was either away sorting out a derailment or else it no longer inhabited the freight engine sidings. It was agreeable to note a spotter toting a camera, for where would the hobby be if photography ceased to play its significant rôle at some time in the future due to a dearth of youngsters carrying on the good work?

Below This shot of 'A4' 60025 *Falcon*, taken from the same spot, stirs up a couple of memories for me. The first is the crowd of keen spotters waiting to watch her couple up to their special excursion. It reminds me of that recent, magnificently nostalgic book *Trainspotting Days* by Will Adams, also published by Silver Link, with it arrays of portraits and studies of spotters, all with apposite captions. My second memory comes up from about sixty-two years ago. Before I owned a camera I borrowed one very briefly on a trip to Grantham where I snapped her as then simply No 25, with stainless steel number plates and tender lettering.

Above Half a century on I can still recall and hear the thrilled cries of the crowd of spotters when the pride of the LNER, *Mallard*, roared southwards through Grantham on a non-stop express. As always she was spotless – I have never seen a photo of her as a 'scruffy duck', though that might not have been the case during the war years of cleaning neglect.

Below This Nottingham-Grantham 'L1'-hauled train seems equally attractive to the line of spotters.

Above Late afternoon, most youngsters had departed for buses or tea in nearby homes. Alone, I watched this graceful 'Pacific' draw to a halt. Very few people boarded or left the train, nor did I notice any loading or unloading of any sort. About three doors slammed to, then the whistle communication between the train's two ends was followed by an electrifying start, the last coach passing me surprisingly soon. Arrival to departure must surely have taken less than a minute. Good platform-work, there!

Above What poor coal! The emission from *Knight of Thistle*'s chimney as he made a rousing northward start was as much felt as smelled. Cinders and unburnt coal rained down upon us through acridity-soaked smoke. Unpleasant? No, not really, for such experiences gladdened the souls of train-watchers of all ages, perhaps particularly so for we older folk, aware that such harmonies of feel, smell and sight would not be with us for much longer.

Right Generally accepted as the best-value-for-money 'Pacifics' on account of the great mileages they could run between major overhauls, the 'A1s' seemed less popular amongst spotters than the 'A3s' and 'A4s' – *St Mungo* lacks an admiring crowd at Grantham, to prove the point. I never discovered why, answers to my queries being merely, 'Just don't like 'em as much' – not particularly forthcoming. They aroused excitement only when they were 'copped'.

Above This bird of non-stop passage swoops through Grantham London-wards, making scarcely a sound until she was flying quite close. Where was the Gresley knock? Had the GWR expertise, applied to much of Gresley stock, silenced this tough, old bird, too?

Below Viewed decades after the shutter clicked, I find it difficult to decide whether the film is responsible for artificially greening the boiler and tender paintwork or whether, in happy fact, 'V2' No 60983 was one of the several Darlington green-painted jobs. At least the spotters seemed impressed by something unusual – or was it just 'a cop' for their stock-books? Although purely fortuitous, the 'copping' syndrome imparted to the number-bagger some sense of self-fulfilment, a kind of harmony between himself, his engines and the stock-book in which the steady accumulation of underlinings afforded cheer and encouragement to pursue the hobby. That stock-book was as closely hugged to the heart as was once The Book of Common Prayer to devout church-goers.

Above This clean 'A3' at Grantham had just been snapped. Ignoring the risk of soon running out of film, a second shot was taken of *Galtee More*, for the balance, the perspective, the harmony of trains passing exerted an irresistible attraction. A secondary factor was involved: very rarely indeed did I shoot British Railways Standard locomotives – the 'Big Four' and their pre-1923 antecedents had the prior claim on my minimal resources in the late summer of 1960, before I started my professional career. Here was my chance to capture a Class 9F without undue waste. I had used this ploy once or twice before – a lovely shot of an LMS Garratt included a passing, almost new Standard Class 5 at Leicester.

Below Saddened by the loss of the pretty, usually well-kept GNR 'C12' 4-4-2T station pilot, I was not a little aggrieved by the terrible external neglect of her replacement, 'N2' 0-6-2T No 69549. She certainly performed adequately, at times fighting with great lengths of stock across sharp curves in the carriage sidings, making quite a smoke-churning racket. One young spotter aims to miss not one single number for he has brought along his dad's binoculars to peer into the distant lines of engines on shed.

Left This photo at Chester was taken mainly on account of the attractive LNWR signal. Surprised by the appearance of the 'Jubilee' – I had expected a 'Mickey' – my endeavour to include both it and the signal proved something of a failure. The signal is there all right, but somewhat beheaded. The LNWR house-style was most obvious in its signal boxes and signals, after its locomotives, of course.

Below A week earlier I had snapped *Princess Elizabeth* parked in the same spot at the head of a fast fitted goods, and with relish I took this later afternoon snap of *Princess Victoria* on similar duty. However, there was a tinge of sadness about the situation. Two 'Royals' on freight service, one sixth of the class, must surely imply severe downgrading prior to withdrawal, for this was in the early 1960s. 'Coronations' were exceedingly rare now in Chester – I had not seen one all day, nor even the week before. That mystic all-inclusive LMS-ishness was being diluted, the harmony invaded by the discordant rumbles, yowlings and horns of diesels. I was glad to scurry into the compartment of my Mold train, still LMS stock and steam-hauled by a Fairburn 2-6-4 tanker.

Above right One of the few success stories in the design-life of Sir Henry Fowler, these long-lap-valve 2-6-4Ts engines were marvels, capable, we are told, of speeds well into the eighties on

fast outer-London suburban services. Hoping against hope became a truth for me, for never once did one take me to or from Mold, despite my fervent wishes – Leicester-Rugby and Leicester-Burton had been my sole unchallenging trips behind them. I sorely wanted to see how one would cope with the demands of Kinnerton Bank, starting from a dead stand at Kinnerton station. This fairly clean example hung around for ages in Chester General before slouching off, coachless, in the direction of Liverpool.

Below Two British Railways Standard Class 5 4-6-0s imprison an LMS 2-6-4T while they all wait to go on shed at Chester. They had been held up by a GWR 'Hall', which had stood fuming with impatience for around 30 minutes to go home. At this distance in time I'm sure the driver or fireman on the nearer loco won't mind me recalling his surreptitious

'pee' in a bucket! Heck – it had been and was going to be a long wait! After the blockading 'Hall' had sped off, before the signalman changed his mind, a further 5 minutes elapsed before the local 'Jinty', shunting like one demented, completed some stock manoeuvres around the station throat, then stopped to gird up his breathless loins. Points slammed, signals clattered and the ensnared trio tore off together – uncoupled – making a crooked bee-line for the sheds. Not at all an uncommon operating mode, for standing on the overbridge by the Manchester lines junction I had frequently seen pairs and trios of engines whipping off to the sheds after a long wait, though many were quite sedate, almost as if savouring, prolonging the ecstasy of having line possession. Or – perish the thought! – were they making a point to the signalmen, expressing their frustrations at being held at bay for so long?

Above A Midland/LMS derivative 4F 0-6-0 slakes its thirst at Chester after a long trek along the testing North Wales coastal route; one assumes that it was not fitted with water pick-up apparatus. Shortly, the driver drew out first his watch, then his pipe and tobacco pouch – just in time to get lit up and relish a few relaxing puffs (as though he didn't inhale enough smoke throughout the working day). I may be wrong, but it seemed to me that drivers preferred the pipe to cigarettes, while young firemen preferred to puff away at 'coffin nails'. That was indeed very noticeable in the platform-end bothy at Leicester Midland station; many a time did I swap pouches with a driver to experiment with different brands and mixtures. 'St Bruno' seemed the commonest choice, with 'Digger Flake' a close second.

Left This engine, seen at Chester and regularly booked for Manchester trains, though never perfectly turned out, never suffered the indignity of complete paintwork neglect that was the fate of one of her sisters glimpsed from time to time at Mold Junction shed, where her duties seemed restricted to freight trains, so attempts at spotlessness would have merely wasted materials, energy and precious time.

Opposite top Glisteningly clean, this first Riddles design for BR looks ready to take over a boat train arriving at Chester from Holyhead. When she set off 20 minutes later, she did so with great gusto yet no wheel-spin. The combined liveries of coach stock and engine were delightful to behold, though neither could ever appear as anything but ultra-drab if neglected for too long.

Right Originating in 1911 on the Midland Railway, the Fowler 4F was the mainstay of freight work throughout the system and eventually took over such haulage after the LMS came into existence in 1923 throughout much of that new company, thanks to the Midlandisation process that saw no fewer than 580 further examples built to top up the already large total of 192 Midland originals. Not the most universally successful 0-6-0, the general outlines of the 4F typify that wheel arrangement, which was a goldmine investment for just about every railway company in British railway history. Our present sample, injector steaming gently away, passes No 46201 *Princess Elizabeth* on its way south through Chester General with a short freight train in 1960.

Right The NER's good old basic, money-earning 0-6-0 is typified here at Gateshead by 'J25' No 65728, an original 1898-built, no-nonsense, saturated-steam-and-slide-valve engine. Sated with indifferent coal but decent water, she slopes off-shed to take up where she left off in her day's duties, while a labour-filthed 'V2' hangs at the back of the queue for a tenderful of coal.

Above left You simply must admire the sheer beauty of this grace-laden NER structure, protecting the up lines and seen in close-up from the overbridge at the outlet of Gateshead shed. Greased and smutty though it was, almost voiceless in operation, it nevertheless called forth my camera to record this fine example of harmony of function and appearance.

Above right One of the footplate crew of 'A3' No 60081 *Shotover* efficiently uses up the long wait in the coaling queue, comprising a 'B1', 'V2' and 'V3', by oiling round. Two hours later I met up once again with this racehorse

namer when she coupled up to a southbound express in Newcastle Central station.

Below What is it about railway layouts that attracts us? Not necessarily the trains that we look forward to watching as they progress along them, it could be the simple fact of their being accurately led in a specific, controlled direction, giving us a sense of orderliness, of regularity of space occupation – something that perhaps satisfies our natural desire for everything to be perfectly directed in our mechanical lives. How often have we stared along a set of empty tracks and

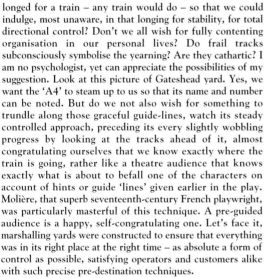

longed for a train – any train would do – so that we could indulge, most unaware, in that longing for stability, for total directional control? Don't we all wish for fully contenting organisation in our personal lives? Do frail tracks subconsciously symbolise the yearning? Are they cathartic? I am no psychologist, yet can appreciate the possibilities of my suggestion. Look at this picture of Gateshead yard. Yes, we want the 'A4' to steam up to us so that its name and number can be noted. But do we not also wish for something to trundle along those graceful guide-lines, watch its steady controlled approach, preceding its every slightly wobbling progress by looking at the tracks ahead of it, almost congratulating ourselves that we know exactly where the train is going, rather like a theatre audience that knows exactly what is about to befall one of the characters on account of hints or guide 'lines' given earlier in the play. Molière, that superb seventeenth-century French playwright, was particularly masterful of this technique. A pre-guided audience is a happy, self-congratulating one. Let's face it, marshalling yards were constructed to ensure that everything was in its right place at the right time – as absolute a form of control as possible, satisfying operators and customers alike with such precise pre-destination techniques.

Above left No matter whether you gaze along the lines of *Harvester* from the front or rear, no annoying protuberances upset the aesthete's eye, nothing suggests disproportion, asymmetry, imbalance. And she was beautifully clean. Gateshead was generally well-reputed for the superb turn-out of engines for the important expresses. I stood close by as the 'Queen of Scots' Pullman set off. The forewarning sound of the blower, the guard's distant, shrill whistle, the acknowledging toot from the front end followed by the sharp 'ffthwump' of the snifting valve excited the ears. Attention was divided between looking up to the cab to watch the regulator being heaved open, then swiftly part-closed to avoid

wheel-slip, and staring at those 6ft 8in driving wheels that crept oh so slowly around their first revolution. The rough grind of metal on metal told of a firm grip on the rails. A few steady exhaust beats, and a light shower of red cinders from the firebox on to the sleepers betokened a clear air-passage for combustion. Wheel-spoke glistenings, coupling-rod flashes in the wan sunshine delighted my eyes as velocity increased. A very minor wheel-slip added sparks at rail level and dark stabs of smoke at chimney height. The sounds were speeding up as each moving part did its job. All too soon the first coaches were tat-tatting past me, replacing the synchronous variety of the noises of a working steam engine. Sight, sound, and smell were sated. I had had a goodly 'fix'.

Above right When I was around the age of this youngster, an ancient, peculiar habit still persisted amongst spotters. It was as though a mystic bond would be made between a locomotive and anyone who touched it, a behaviour bordering on superstition. In general, 'cabbing' was regarded as the ultimate pride-creating fulfilment for any spotter, something to boast about. I recall seeing the word 'cabbed' entered at the side of underlined numbers in quite a few religiously regarded stock-books in the 1940s and early 1950s. Certainly, the touching, the magical contact, was readily observed at any important rail centre to which a pilgrimage had been made, an act akin to that of kissing the outer casket of a saint's remains, his statue or portrait, just as devoutly practised today by fervent Roman Catholics and Greek Orthodox adherents. Did I, too, likewise indulge myself in this quasi-religious worship? I would like to think so, to be able to think that I had not missed out on one of the ineluctable mystiques of those years of juvenile trainspotting. It came as quite a tingling shock to behold at Newcastle that the practice was still followed as late as 1959. Such conduct had entirely passed out my memory decades ago. Quite a touching reminder.

Above One day, chilled and tea-longing, I deserted Gateshead for Newcastle Central station, and a near immaculate original Raven 'B16', No 61429, was the first thing I clapped eyes on as I made my way along the southbound platform. Just as serious conversation stops abruptly and is cast aside when a young child pops into a room of debating adults, so did the serious business of hot tea and a thorough warm-up evaporate from my thoughts. She was hauling an immense load, but surely well within her capacity since she was classified one power group higher than the 'Black Fives' – namely Class 6. Her curvaciousness was fully mind-holding in itself – superior in lineament to any of the Gresley or Thompson rebuilds, even without the adornment of LNWR-style paintwork and lining-out. No matter from which angle she was studied she was eye-catching, that long-boiler so well proportioned and thus not

suggestive of that gangliness that spoils other long-boilered small-wheeled engines, as in the case of the LNWR 'Super D'. 'Beauty is as beauty does' came to mind when she set off from the signal halt. Her departure was without wheel-slip or fuss, getting steadily into her stride with sharp exhaust blasts reminiscent of those of a GWR 'Hall'. So passed perhaps a full minute of visually studying a stationary beauty, augmented shortly afterwards by a graceful departure. I wondered whether she was the last Raven 'B16' to receive a full overhaul *and* immaculate paintwork in Darlington Works. Had the stalwart remnants of ex-NER staff thereby sent off a 'living', sparkling memorial to finally remind the world of the greatness and glory of the North Eastern Railway's motive power? After all, steam was well and truly on its way out, causing countless engines to struggle on with minimal general overhaul, let alone paintwork.

Left Surely the point is enforced by my contrasting shot, taken but half an hour later. The lineaments of this rebuild are indeed far from ugly, but even allowing for its ditched-in grime, the nigh slinky grace of the original Raven shows how carefully the gracious Edwardian engine had been designed with as much attention paid to aesthetics as to mechanical efficiency. The rebuilds placed efficiency and ease of service access to moving parts well ahead of appearance considerations. Audibly, visually, as she heaved her grime-loaded bulk off to Gateshead MPD, she was equally alluring as her shine-laden sister – sharp exhaust and silky motion.

Above 'Mystic harmony' here takes on a different meaning for the train-watcher, with an example of the mysteries of complex and intense signal and route control. All three trains were moving across the maze of tracks at the north end of Newcastle Central station. 'Keeping your eye on the balls', so to speak, was a huge responsibility for the signalmen, for hesitancy would lead to delays, thereby causing upsets in the route-planning of the box in the next section. Behind me, just departing northwards, was an Edinburgh train, while I could hear the snorts of a through freight behind the station wall – five trains to be synchronously, harmoniously guided along their own ways, none obstructing another's path, a masterly achievement to be continuously repeated hour in, hour out by the signalmen.

Right Although a delicious viewpoint covering all the lines through the station and across the bridges to Gateshead sheds, I rarely had the chance to take advantage of the castle keep at Newcastle, but when I did I

marvelled at the perspective, the harmonic flowing of the tracks into, across and around each other. The glisten of sunlight on polished steel rail was akin to fine artwork done with the eye of a draughtsman. No train could be missed, nor locos running light on or off shed. At platform level the multi-complex train workings, interweavings and so on appeared mind-boggling, indeed nightmarish at times. Seen from high up, as though from a god-like control-perch, the manoeuvres were immediately comprehensive and the slickness and organisational abilities of the signalmen highly appreciated. Shunting now made sense, apparent hold-ups were not truly such, but a part of an overall strategy to get as many trains to where they had to go with no or minimal disruption to any other particular train. There were occasional queues on the through freight lines, but they were always dealt with expeditiously. Below me we see an ex-NER 0-6-0 trundling along with its trail of coal hoppers – noisy things they were indeed when empty.

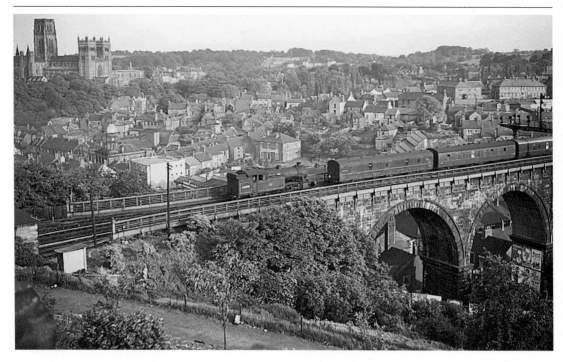

Above These scenes are taken from the castellations on the top section of the Wharton Gardens at Durham, which afforded me a happy though but very occasional rare treat with or without a camera. This elevated viewpoint harmonised for me three valued 'institutions': the high-perched, glorious Norman cathedral – symbolising my cathedral upbringing and love of music – the equally perched castle – my university 'home' for many years of study and sport – and finally the ever-rewarding railway scene – an enthralling hobby and utterly essential source of wage packets earned each vacation.

Efficient usage of engines, the avoidance of having them stand idle, is illustrated by the Gresley 'V1' and 'V3' tanks based in Durham, though not shedded there. In between hauling branch trains to Sunderland and Bishop Auckland, they were called upon to bank heavy southbound passenger trains across the rising, curving viaduct. Parcels and mail trains at times of substantial weight would also call for assistance after stopping. The 2-6-2T never went further than a hundred yards beyond the signal gantry along the viaduct. Sight and sound were the predominant senses aroused when trains got under way: acrid sky-high smoke

would bring the olfactory sense into play when the load was mighty and the rails wet.

Below Degree studies finished, time was suddenly plentiful, but money was not. No holiday trip for me – thoughts about the future were essential. What nicer than sitting in long grass on a sunny slope just watching the passage of clouds against blue skies and smoky steam against cutting sides while turning over in the mind those seemingly big questions that face any new graduate? As recorded in my earlier book, one must switch off intense questioning and relax in an all-absorbing hobby to free up the mind, to allow it to steadily produce non-frantic answers. The ideal location for me was this field overlooking the railway and overrun by turkeys (which also added to the essential distraction process, though far less so than the steam trains and occasional snapshot-taking. This 'B1' has managed to heave its great length of freight wagons off the wheel-dragging curve of Durham Viaduct, its fireman now shovelling into the firebox what, judging by the exhaust, is not coal of the best steam quality.

I recall how much I felt at one with myself, how much I enjoyed following that common-or-garden filth-coated 'B1'

until it was out of sight, though not out of hearing, for a few hundred yards further south the line entered a deep, echoing, stone-faced cutting. That 'B1' had afforded me several minutes of simple companionship, while reminding me that not many days hence I would meet several of her sisters when I donned the labouring garb of carriage-cleaner and general dogsbody at Leicester Belgrave Road station. I winced at the coming unpleasantness, which offset the brighter moments in that GNR backwater.

11
NIGHT SHOTS

'And in the night-season also I take no rest'
Psalm 22

I would not blame my cameras – should they be given the power of speech – for plaintively echoing the words of the psalmist, since, after being regularly lugged and bounced around in briefcase, coat-pocket, saddlebag and rucksack, or slung from heaving shoulders, any camera should be entitled to some respite. No such consideration for my apparatus – I was a hard task-master. The steam railway becomes all the more awesome during 'the night-season', when chiller air, condensing whatever steam escapes, wreathes and whirls it around the locomotive in a magic aura made all the more intense by its starkness against a black sky as it dances with its nocturnal partners – station lamps and signal glimmers.

Night-shift railway work, and many a late journey to and from university, immersed me in that ethereal ambience numerous times each year.

Even when utterly exhausted, nearing the end of a sinew-cracking portering shift in the early hours, I would watch the newspaper train romp into Leicester Central station, my spirit thereby refreshed and uplifted by the sight of shafts of station lights scampering across the engine, cheerfully co-mingling their stabs and caresses with the seemingly more leisurely turmoils of steam from chimney, safety-valve, woebegone glands and leaky carriage-heating hoses. The diaphanous dreaminess of such beauty could last but a fleeting few seconds before the grinding of the final brake application brought it to an end, my feet now hurrying to my designated parcel van, my hands anticipating the stark chill of the long brassy bar to be uplifted to gain access to the mountains of newspapers that would bruise with their weight and awkward shape, cut with the string bindings and – final hurt – stain hands with printer's ink. Trolleys high-stacked above our heads, pulled away from the coach and van sides,

Leicester Central witnessed the massive influx of 'B1' 4-6-0s once the originating company's motive power had been scrapped – classes 'B3' to 'B9' were soon extinct once the wartime need of them had gone, although not before I had seen them at work. No doubt the Thompson substitutes were superior, which went some way towards compensating for their less graceful lines. No 1038 *Umseke* was a favourite local hero, so to speak, though rarely cleaned up, it seemed. Seemingly ever-present No 61188 is parked in the south bay of Leicester Central ready to take over a Sheffield-London train late one November evening. Its firebox glow accompanied by the cheery lights of Leicester South signal box conspired to make my bones more aware of the starkly chilly air coursing through the high-up, exposed station.

the dream-scene might be resumed, for 'The Newspaper', tightly scheduled, would set off northwards amidst still broader sheaths of gyrating, urgently throbbing, skyward-bellowing fields of steam and smoke than had heralded its arrival amongst us, whilst whispering wisps gently soughed past us as every leaking heating hose caressed our legs with their gentle 'farewell till tomorrow' kisses. Somehow, the sight of literally tons of newspapers to be hauled down below and loaded for the local distributors to collect seemed less daunting as I snatched a last very few seconds to watch the tail-lamp glimmer, then dwindle within its light halo of reddish steam.

Above For years I was proud of this nocturnal Leicester GCR shed scene. My very first, very primitive camera served me amazingly well that night. A pile of bricks for some repair or new construction work stood ready and waiting to support Mr Kershaw Penguin – the camera – whose wretchedly small aperture of f11, abetted by very slow film (all I could afford as a fourteen-year-old) exacted an 8-minute time exposure. My Decembral-frozen fingers were kept crossed to exorcise any attempt by drivers to move the 'B1s', the lurking 'A3' and its side-kick 'V2' out of the shed. The ritual worked.

Footplate crews and labourers passed by me, asking not whether I permission to trespass, but did I really think the photo would turn out. The greatest surprise of all was the railway policeman who had silently come up for a chat about our shared hobby – photography. Thus were those 8 minutes happily spent, in spite of the intense cold, which caused even my goose-pimples to huddle together for warmth.

Below The encounter with the policeman encouraged me to linger for further shots. 'O4/7' No 63860, one of the few fitted with an 'O2' Class boiler, squeaked into the shed yard. Footplate staff descending and going indoors suggested that the engine would not be moving for several minutes. Resting the camera on the top of a yard telephone box, I took a time exposure, during which No 65495, our resident 'J5', decided to join the portrait. Parked without obscuring the 2-8-0, whose rear had been exposed to the camera for perhaps a minute, the 0-6-0 stayed put for 3 minutes, thereby adding locomotive interest to the photo while creating the eerie ethos of a ghostly haunting – you can see right through her!

Above No 60049 *Galtee More* replaced the two freight locos, who shortly sauntered off, the 'O4' still squeaking. I love this scene, which includes the water-crane with its dripping water and tipsy brazier, plenty of smoke and some steam.

Right 'B1s' galore were available that night. Two decent examples stood stock still for the time exposure, which recorded the essential flare lamp's progress and also a pleasant halo from the overhead yard lamp.

Right Daringly entering the shed, I espied No 61326 dead and cold. She couldn't move during a time exposure! But where to stand the camera? Only one place, on the rails of the next track – hence the very low angle.

Above A chill December evening did not deter me from attempting time exposures at Leicester Central sheds with my primitive camera and dreadfully slow film. 'A3' No 60052 *Prince Palatine* has just emerged from inside the shed in the wake of a 'B1' 4-6-0. Both moved off within thirty minutes, the latter seen heading south with a few coaches. The 'Prince' I did not see, so assumed he wandered northwards.

Below   Interesting photographs could result from unavoidably lengthy time exposures. 'A3' No 60102 had rolled into Leicester GC shed after bringing the down 'Master Cutler' as far as Central station. The flare lamp used by the engine disposal personnel is traced over a period of 8 minutes, moving from the footplate forwards and ending up at the smokebox, whose door was then opened and ashes shovelled out. Today, of course, such photos are never taken – fast films, fast lenses or flash guns have seen to that.

Right Back in the first half of the 1950s I had elected to travel home from the North East via the LNWR, joining it at Carlisle. Needless to say, several hours were spent at Citadel station, never having had the delights of that marvellous location within camera-range. Always preferring the Rugby rather than the Nuneaton connection for Leicester, it was nightfall when I detrained at the former just in time to get a hand-held short-time-exposure shot of the 'Deltic' prototype in original livery as it paused on its way northwards. It was surrounded by official-looking folk, so I had to wait until all were back on the footplate – sorry, in the cab!

That left just one photographic bullet to fire through the glass barrel of my hard-worked camera. A 'Mickey', No 44909, grunted to a halt at the far end of the station towards which I was ambling in search of a cup of tea. There was just sufficient light for a time exposure of around 5 seconds, the camera perched on a trolley of postal sacks – which reminded me that next day I would be heaving tons of those abrasive, skin-searing objects at Leicester Midland station. ('Sign on at 1.45, lad!')

Below Acrid air assaulted eyes and lungs of passengers in the days of Glasgow's suburban steam, all the more when in a confined area such as Glasgow Central's Low Level station. I had wandered in after a late winter's afternoon at openly fresh-aired Queen Street station, and the contrast could not have been greater. A quick shot of the Fairburn and BR 2-6-4 tanks for the record, and up and out I went. My cowardice was shortly punished, for my return train to Edinburgh was a measly, out-of-sorts diesel railcar, whose odours proved less acceptable than those of the Low Level station.

Above Trudging back from Princes Street station to Waverley to return to Durham after a hectic day's outing to Edinburgh and Glasgow, I knew that one exposure remained in my camera. Ten minutes before my 'A3'-headed train was due to leave I spotted a reasonably lit 'B1', far better in fact than my be-shadowed 'A3' – hence the portrait of No 61356, which was destined for the Waverley route. Life is added to the nocturnal scene by the watching porter and guard, complete with hand-lamp.

Below I have always had a soft spot for the 'B17' Class, no doubt due to my very early acquaintance with them on the GCR line, but the advent of a fleet of 'B1s' and the return of the 'A3' 'Pacifics' to that line ousted them. It was to be a long time before I was reunited with them, the occasion being a far too brief call at King's Cross in 1951, when an almost clean class member dropped in with a train from Cambridge. A 1-second time-exposure was made by leaning my camera for slight support against a trolleyful of cardboard boxes. No time to indulge in close examination was possible – there was the last train to catch from St Pancras next door, and a mere 10 minutes left to get on board.

Above A disappointing night visit to Liverpool Street station – high hopes of securing atmospheric shots of a 'B12', a 'B17', a 'D16' or one of the 2-4-2 tanks were thwarted. Not even a 'B1' rolled up, despite a 45-minute wait. I had to be satisfied with this 4-minute exposure of an 'N7', during the last minute of which a 'Britannia' eased in to couple up to some coaches – it is just discernible in the background. Moving swiftly to reach its platform I was nevertheless defeated, for scarcely was I through the ticket barrier when the flag was waved, the green light shown (why both? I wondered), a hoot from the engine and away went the train, unphotographed.

Below Across the river at London's Victoria station, No 30483, an 'H15' 4-6-0 of LSWR origin, has arrived with a boat train, which somewhat surprised me since I believed that they were never called upon for such arduous duties.

Left No 35021 *New Zealand Line* came into Victoria shortly afterwards, though not with a boat train. She stayed an inordinately long time at the buffer stops – probably no carriage pilot was available to remove her stock.

Left 'Schools' No 30928 *Stowe* crept in so slowly. Was there a newly appointed driver at the regulator, taking extra care until he was fully confident with his braking skills?

Below 'E1' 4-4-0 No 31067, a Maunsell rebuild of a Wainwright 'E' 4-4-0, contrasts with the previous engine in all respects other than wheel arrangement – inside cylinders, un-named, no smoke defectors and noticeably in a very grubby state. Still, it was delightful to study a less than modern locomotive for several minutes.

Right Unless one is a student of mediaeval literature, its romances in particular, the vast majority of the 'King Arthur' Class names convey nothing. A typical example is No 30781 *Sir Aglovale*, who has just galloped into his London fortress conveying, perhaps, more than one damsel in distress. Tethered behind him, his steely stallion is taking on water from one of the many supply pipes.

Right and below Two classic 4-4-0s within 30 minutes was quite unexpected, even at Waterloo. To the left of LSWR 'T9' No 30718, the blurred outline of a trolley handle reveals that the exposure was made with the camera perched atop some luggage or parcels. The beautiful Wainwright No 31586 was taken with a hand-held half-second shot.

Left and below left An orchestral concert had attracted me from Mold into Chester one wintry Saturday. Feeling incompletely dressed without a camera when travelling by train, I had stuffed my 'rough job' Baldinette into my top-coat pocket. A solid Brahms and Delius concert having thrilled me, I returned to the station to catch the last train back. The platform clock advised me that I had ample time to saunter and seek something on which to expose film. A GWR 'Castle' and a Stanier 8F 2-8-0 were on offer, the former being the better illuminated – a 2-second exposure hopefully recorded her. Turning my attention to the 8F, a 3-minute exposure was assessed as being sufficient. My calculation was wrong. I got a negative all right, but a thin one that did not print up too well, whereas that of the 'Castle' was satisfactory. In years to come I was glad of that concert, for it had led me to take my sole night exposure of a 'Castle'. Yes, there has always been a mystical link between railways and music, a peculiarity more fully dealt with in *A Friend in Steam*.

Right I had badly chosen a night to attempt time exposures in Newcastle Central station, and on reaching the exposed heights of Durham station I walked into heavy rain. Uncomfortable for the photographer indeed, but the rain-covered platforms acting as reflectors added fifty per cent more illumination to the 'A8' 4-6-2 tank, waiting for the connecting express from London, to carry passengers on to Sunderland. Thus a short hand-held exposure just, only just, sufficed to capture the scene.

With less than a month before the total closure of the Ruabon-Barmouth route, I set off with camera and primitive flash equipment one Saturday afternoon, reaching the latter station after dusk. A few poor shots were taken in the station before I decided to try my hand at moving flash photography. A few words with the crew of the train pictured here advised them not be startled by photographic flashing – they were not in the least concerned. Off I walked, crossed the famous bridge and waited. My film stock was not of the fastest then available, nor were the flash-

bulbs very powerful, yet two reasonably printable negatives were made. I was pleased with myself, but not with the authorities, who had decided to shut down and rip up the lovely scenic route along which I travelled back to Wrexham an hour or so later. That line well illustrated the beautifying influence of the railway on the surrounding countryside, the gracious curves, cuttings and embankments, bordered with self-setting trees. Seen from near or far, the blend of man and nature was satisfyingly attractive. A trip along the line did the mind a power of good.

Above With drain cocks opened to full blast, an 'A2' sets off from Newcastle Central with an Edinburgh train. The racket she made was doubled by the echo from the close-by stone wall. I had elected to photograph further away than usual to avoid getting nothing but the shafts of steam that would be enveloping the engine. Also, distance allowed me to use a slow shutter speed of a mere quarter-second, just enough to freeze movement.

Below The 2-6-2 tank was badly sited for a night shot – too much wreathed in steam. Luckily the problem was resolved when a 'J39' 0-6-0 slowly rumbled into decent light. She was snapped with the 'V3' and her parcels stock included as an almost off-stage extra. This was great luck, for it was very rarely that a freight tank passed between the passenger platforms at Newcastle instead of travelling behind the stone-walled by-pass.

12
MISCELLANY

Whenever I show my photo albums of steam railways to fellow enthusiasts, it comes as something of a surprise to them to perceive apparent chaos: nothing is orderly, there are no themes, no sections dedicated to specific types, places, dates and so forth. But surely, I suggest to them, that is precisely how we experienced our steam railway days, darting here and there, stumbling across new spotting places, deliberately planning excursions or blindly setting off on a cycle tour wondering where we could end up, what we might see and so on.

'I wonder what picture we shall see when we turn the page' incites anticipation. Similarly, but within stricter limits, a strong element of 'I wonder what we shall see today' always impinged on our thinking, on our hopeful anticipations as we settled down at the lineside, on a bridge or a station bench. In broad terms we had a pretty good idea of what to expect, especially along the main lines, though in what order was not fully foreseeable: expecting an 'A4' on the 'Flying Scotsman' I was twice surprised to see it drawn by a 'V2'; on both occasions the 'Pacific' had failed and been replaced at Peterborough. 'V2's had, of course, been expected and, indeed, a good score or more passed in the course of the day, together with at least a dozen 'A4s' as wished for.

Doing a spot of spotting along that long-time favourite haunt, the 'Black Pad', mentioned elsewhere, I knew that a 'K2' would pass by at some time, probably on a fish train. One indeed did, but on the close-by LMS line coming from Burton-on-Trent with a four-coach all-stations train – utterly unpredictable, a near impossibility for such an appearance! That afternoon the fast fish galloped past behind a 'B16' – equally a most rare surprise.

My earliest photographs – always in small sets of eight roll-film contact prints – were carefully mounted, in correct sequence, in small, cheap albums, details scrupulously written underneath.

Eventually, as the collection swelled in proportion to the amount of money and travel availability, I began to find that each logical presentation – place, date, engine, etc – handy though it was as an aide-memoire – gave the impression of being a fossilised collection, each section akin, so to speak, to an immutable geological stratum. I experimented by juggling around the contents of one album with my eyes averted. The outcome was surprising, most refreshing, for instead of knowing what was on the next page before turning it, I was transported to an entirely different location, period and locomotive type, recovering that many-years-before excitement that had accompanied and preceded the taking of each particular photograph. A secondary benefit was the exercise it gave the old grey cells and their memory capabilities. The mild memory 'shock' stirred up otherwise forgotten details surrounding the occasion when the photograph had been taken, be they about the weather or the detailed conversation with a railwayman.

When writing A Friend in Steam, it was the photograph of the Belgrave Road Station signal box that reminded me of the semi-profound discussion I had had with signalman Henry half a century ago about the mysteries of the rate of the passage of time through our personal lives. I had been idly flipping through a disparate album. A scene of distant-place-and-period had been looked at, then the page was turned to reveal Leicester Belgrave Road GNR box. Plentiful memories re-surged until my generally fine recall threw up the impressive conversation, which also suited my point in the book about the high intelligence of a vast proportion of steam days railwaymen.

In the interest of cohesion, the present publication has been sectionalised. However, this particular section, 'Miscellany', allows me to flit around the realm of my negatives with negligible groupings or classifications, as in the set of scenes at Chester and its environs, for example. Thus you, too, will flit from an ex-Midland Railway 3F near Kirby Muxloe to an ex-LB&SCR 'C2X' at Lewes, then off north to contemplate an ex-Caledonian Railway 2F on Stirling shed, its caption containing my views on the ubiquitous 0-6-0 wheel arrangement to form a very tenuous incidental link between these three scenes, while the individual captions remain totally pertinent to each individual picture.

Was it not true of all of us steam-lovers that we wandered far and near every weekend, yearly garnering memories and photographs in an attempt to stock them up and thus in a way to possess the railway's mystique? However, when looking back with a friend over any year's (or more) accumulation, the memories do not emerge in exact time and/or place sequence. Thus:

'Do you remember that day on Stoke Bank when we saw nineteen "A4s"?' (A trip in 1953)

'Ah yes, just as delightful as that brilliantly sunny day spent at Atherstone when we saw "Coronations" in three different liveries three years ago!' (A trip in 1950)

'And I was so lucky on the way there to get that shot of the "Super D" on the Nuneaton-Loughborough line!' (Ditto 1950)

'That reminds me! I want to check on the "A4s" we saw two years ago in Scotland, cos they may be the only ones we didn't see on Stoke Bank, which means we might have seen every English-shedded "A4" in just one day! Fantastic!' (Scottish tour 1954 mixed with cycle day-trip 1953)

'I've just got back my cine films of Southam Road & Harbury. When I've edited them together you must pop round and see them as well as the shots around Sunderland and Durham that you didn't see last year. Good excuse for a pot of tea, anyway.'

That is how the following selection is presented. The mildly mystical but unplanned mixings of time, place, engine types, dates and comments should not, I hope, prove a discordant but rather a harmonious agglomeration of my numerous, happy steam-haunted moments.

Below One of my earliest and favourite snapshots. My preference in Midland 2P 4-4-0s has always been for the originals of 1891-1901, though not for their historical significance. While 3½ inches does not seem a large differentiation in wheel diameter, in appearance the more 'leggy' 7ft 0½in Midland originals are better proportioned in relationship to the engine's overall stature than are their later 1928-29 LMS 6ft 9in descendants. I support my contention with this shot of No 40410 at Leicester Midland station. I wonder if the school-capped spotter has maintained his interest in railways.

Above right The 0-6-0 tanks throughout Britain, humble creatures in the eyes of most spotters, were of nigh immeasurable value to their owing companies, for their work in marshalling yards was essential for the efficient sorting and despatching of the vast quantities of freight that were the life-blood of every railway system. This ex-Caledonian Railway McIntosh 2F was continuously busy in the yards at Inverness. The photograph was taken deliberately to include the fine signal gantry just outside the station.

Below right I was delighted to meet ex-LB&SCR 'Remembrance' Class member No 32329 for the second time. Two years earlier my roll of film had been badly processed, resulting in a 'furry' set of negatives. Cycling once again through Basingstoke, my wheels turned – as if drawn by the incantatory magic sounds of an engine shed – towards the depot. My frustration-loaded remembrance of a shoddy negative of *Stephenson* dissolved alongside the steam from a nearby 'T9' (No 30119) as I looked beyond it to behold the ideally positioned 'N15X' 4-6-0. Every care was taken over focus and exposure to produce this, to me, classic portrait.

Above 'Low, he comes with clouds descending!' How easy it was to appositely appropriate those hymn words! Dawlish sea-front was – is – a spotters' heaven. Back in 1951 my primitive Kershaw Penguin camera was capable of producing reasonable photographs if I did not demand too much of it. Happily No 6830 *Buckenhill Grange* was just trickling along, slowly enough for my miserably slow shutter to cope. Equally fortunate was the following wind creating a down-waft of smoke, lovely to look at and, in its way, intoxicating to inhale.

Below A long pedal from Gloucester had brought me to Monmouth (Troy) in time to snap an auto-train within seconds of its departure down-river. Well patronised, it certainly needed strengthening with an extra coach. Activity in the neighbouring goods yard strongly suggested that business was far better than stated in the reasons for the Wye Valley line closure just a few short years later.

Top Doncaster Works, our club was informed, looked after its staff well, to the extent of running trains for them from the station to 'The Plant'. We were directed to look in one of the station bays where, in truth, there stood a 'J52' 0-6-0 saddle tank at the head of a motley mix of clean but ancient-looking ex-GNR coaching stock – one or two bogies ahead of a few six-wheelers. Since we had permits to visit at least the sheds, I asked if we could avail ourselves of the next departure, for time was as short as the wintry day. A firm refusal was the response.

Middle I have often wondered why should there be a mystique about engine numbers ending in two noughts. In the NRM's magnificent collection of locomotives there stands Class 5 No 5000. More than once I have heard youngsters exult over the 'roundness' – for want of a better word – of such numbers. Well, to delight those so entranced I offer No 65300, a former North British Railway 'J36' 0-6-0 sitting docilely behind Haymarket shed wall. I, personally, felt not in the least bewitched by the number!

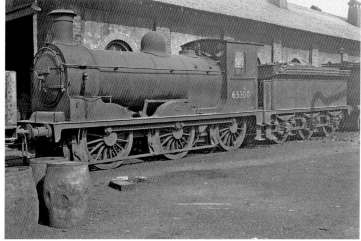

Bottom No 53804, an S&DJR 2-8-0, stands waiting her turn for shopping in Derby Works. Ahead of her is a line of Stanier 8Fs, which, we were informed, had just returned from service overseas, now needing to be rehabilitated into the BR system, for they had certain extra fittings superfluous to British needs together with some modifications unapparent to us. Our guide was unsure whether they came from Turkey or Iraq. We never did find out – it could have been neither.

Above Many were the named express trains run by the Western Region. A brief respite from pedalling along the South Wales coast was taken in Newport, and where else but on the station! Tea and a bun were as excellent as the weather – lightly clouded sun suits black-and-white steam photography. The 'Pembroke Coast Express' was immaculate, headed by a healthy sounding *Llandovery Castle*, thrilling me with a fast traverse of the station on the through line.

Below Long-abandoned Scalford station and it signal box silently watch the passage of an 'Austerity' with its lengthy freight train heading south along the old GN&LNW Joint line from Nottingham. We had waited ages for a train in order to have some record of this line. About to leave, we were approached by a swift-striding signalman who had left his box specifically to advise us to hang on for a little longer. We did, and captured this now nostalgic scene. The GNR 'somersault' starter signal, just visible beyond the box, was permanently fixed after the cessation of passenger services – no need for it, of course, since freight simply did not stop in the station, especially on account of the facing gradient.

Above We all have a soft spot (non-steam fans would say 'our heads'!) for the amiable little local train, all the more so should it be an auto-train. Before the Beeching 'bash-it-all-up' sessions, there were numerous such trains serving both remote and urban areas right across Britain, though there were proportionately fewer in Scotland. A delicious intimacy entwined them with the surrounding scenery, rural or in town. We have all noticed, say, tourists with no interest whatsoever in railways looking up to watch the wee train pass, and in all likelihood pass approving comments. These trains added visual life to sparsely populated areas, seeming determined to dispel their moribund ethos with sound, movement, smoke and steam. Regular passengers, guard and footplate staff become a mobile family, happy in one another's company, passing news, leg-pulling. Perhaps you have heard of the daily travelling season-ticket holder on one such train who one day forgot his ticket. The guard, on his ticket inspection round, was told, 'My face is my ticket,' to which he replied, 'Then I'd better punch it!'

Yes, indeed, those were the days. Only once did I travel along the Rugby-Leamington line – such a beautiful, pastoral route then, but sadly in my pre-camera-toting days. Waiting to snap the 'Royal Scot' heading out of Rugby Midland I was fortunate to see and bag 2-6-2T No 41228 snappily setting off for Leamington, promptly reviving memories of that one journey, years before.

Below Just south of Rugby Midland there was a field overlooking the main line and the various junctions connecting it with Market Harborough and Northampton. Hiding the station from view – to the annoyance of some spotters – was the superb structure of the Great Central's girder bridge across which 'Pacifics' and lesser locos rattled from time to time. Too distant for any hope of a successful, frame-filling picture of a train using the bridge, one prayed that a train would cross it just as a train was snapped on the ex-LNWR tracks. I was lucky – just once! As I was shooting a 'British Railways'-lettered 'Crab' setting off for Northampton with a set of Stanier suburban stock, an ex-GCR 'Pom-Pom' 'J11' cleared the cage of girders sufficiently to be included in the picture, working a Rugby-Nottingham local.

Above I was on my way to Worcester to discover a different part of the GWR system. Snack-wolfing time conveniently made itself apparent as I reached Stratford-upon-Avon, right by the station, too! There is nothing special about the loco or the location, but the picture reminds me of the most satisfying feeling I enjoyed there: I felt fit, I had ridden forty miles or so non-stop, I was munching away on a simple yet tasty snack, the weather was kindly, then along came this GWR 2-8-0 to complete my satisfaction. It seemed to be the final element that set the seal on the entire few joyous minutes with its sounds, its purposeful movement, its emanation of power... My body had needed the sandwiches' vitamins to keep me functioning. The soul, the mind, call it

what you will, needed the 'vitamins' of utter contentment that, in this instance, assuredly would have been inadequate without the passing presence of a steam train. Mystic harmony? Indeed!

Below Much of the visually mystic harmony before nationalisation in 1948 resulted from the 'house style' of each company, though these were further subdivided into the house styles of the pre-1923 companies. Regret would be felt when a pre-1923 engine was photographed in its 'birth territory', but whose signals had been replaced by modern standard versions. The GWR, eminently a self-contained entity as regards house style, could always be relied upon to

furnish the photographer with one of its engines surrounded by GWR infrastructure and accessory equipment. This 1952 picture at Leamington Spa shows a totally GWR scene – apart from the livery, the engine (No 4083 *Abbotsbury Castle*), coaches and signals are pure ex-GWR.

Right Passenger services had ceased on the West Bridge to Burton line way back in the 1930s, yet the stations en route were kept in just passable good order since offices were still needed for the paperwork of the heavy coal traffic, supplemented by meagre general merchandise. Glenfield station was an example, partially included in this shot of 2F No 58264 passing through with coal empties for the West Leicestershire mines.

Below This is one of my most cherished photos. 'Why? It's only a 2P,' you ask. 2Ps have always been attractive engines and I endeavoured many times to take photographs that showed their grace and power to best advantage. In my opinion, this was as close to success as I could hope to attain, given my not-of-the-best-quality camera. The slight gradient out of Syston Junction, together with the curve, demanded a rigorous departure, always producing excellent smoke effects and plenty of noise. Non-stop up trains were unbothered by the mild gradient, consequently providing very little smoke.

Top It was not worth the bother and undoubted expense of setting up machine tooling, etc, to build just one pair of 0-4-2 tank engines, so the Great North of Scotland Railway ordered them from Manning Wardle in 1915 as Class 'Z4'. Their raison d'être was shunting the sharply curved Aberdeen quays. A slightly more powerful version ('Z5') followed the same year, with driving wheels 6 inches greater in diameter and with cylinders increased by 1 inch in length.

Any difference that a mere additional 160lb of tractive effort may have made is dubious, though on the other hand the additional 10 tons' adhesion weight was a decided advantage, assuming that most of it was via the driving wheels (5 tons per axle), with a negligible amount on the trailing pony-truck. The first of the 'Z4s', No 68190, is busy on the task for which she was created – shunting fish wagons on Aberdeen's quays.

Middle 'Common or garden' is a well-used term. In the case of the 0-6-0 wheel arrangement, I prefer to transmute it into 'Common, all garden', for it grew, it flourished as has no other wheel arrangement in every acre of all railway companies' territory before nationalisation ousted it with 'Moguls', tender and tank versions. Even the Great North of Scotland Railway ran a few before settling on 4-4-0s and 0-4-2 tanks only. No 57441, an ex-Caledonian Railway 2F of 1883, finely illustrates my point, for it was performing well and economically, despite its age. Designed in 1883, these 2Fs gave stalwart service and must have handsomely repaid their construction price and subsequent maintenance costs by the time this sample was photographed on Stirling shed in 1954 – seventy years of reliability. Dugald Drummond did a fine job on them, for Lambie and McIntosh perpetuated the class, bringing the total to 222. They were out-numbered only by the combined Midland Railway and LMS 4Fs, 192 of the former and no fewer than 580 of the latter, 772 in all. Multi-purpose 0-6-0s, these Caledonians worked passenger trains quite regularly, 102 of them permanently fitted with Westinghouse brakes.

Bottom Arriving in 1954 at Newhaven after an exhausting hitch-hiking tour around Europe (I still have a sunburned thumb to prove it), a change of trains had to be made at Lewes. Waiting for the London train I cast around for some Southern steam, but saw none until, seconds before the London train arrived, this ex-LB&SCR 'C2X' strolled in with some oldish stock. A swift shot and the vision was gone, for my London electric train cut across it. I wondered if the rebuild from Class 'C2' was really worth the time and money, for there was but a miserly increase in boiler pressure of 10lb (160 to 170), yielding an increase in tractive effort of but 1,125lb. Adhesion weight might have been the goal, for weight rose from 39 to 45 tons – 2 extra tons per pair of driving wheels. One thing about our hobby is its comprehensive

involvement of all our faculties, in this present instance simple mathematical calculations, leading to an evaluation of the merits of rebuilding a particular class of engine. I looked, I photographed, I checked details, I did some basic maths, then – this is the important part – I *thought* about it, I queried its worth. Steam railway study did, and still does, have a harmonising influence on us, though mere number-bagging, in my opinion, despite having its own (limiting) mystique, involving little more than looking and noting, does not and cannot bring many of our mind's skills into harmonious, satisfying play.

Right It was not unusual for a 3F 0-6-0 to fill in time between coal trains with Leicester-Burton passenger trains. Here we see one just after leaving Kirby Muxloe with an evening service from Burton. Regular motive power was either a 2P 4-4-0 or a Fowler 2-6-4T. However, I have seen a 'Black Five', a 'Crab' (and once, a Caprotti version), a 4F 0-6-0, several 4P Compounds, a Stanier 2-6-4T and, on a bizarre occasion, an LNER 'K2' 'Mogul'. I suspect they were on 'filling-in' diagram workings, the 'K2' perhaps being 'borrowed' after it had worked into Burton either from the ex-GNR Stafford line or from Derby Friargate.

Below At first sight a double-headed four-coach train seems a ridiculously wasteful exercise. In this instance the late afternoon Leicester to Burton-on-Trent train, always hauled by a 2P, was assisted by BR Standard 2-6-2T No 84008, which was merely working her passage back home, there

being no service on which she could be used. This also saved on block working for the signalmen, and avoided the slight problem of fitting a light engine path into the line's working timetable. The duo is caught near Desford, just where the original Leicester & Swannington line from West Bridge joined the Midland Railway's later route from Wigston Junction to Burton, an essential construction, for Glenfield Tunnel, on the old line, was far too narrow and shallow a bore to permit up-to-date loco and coaching stock, quite apart from the impossibility of fitting passenger train times into those of the slow-moving, frequently stopping, pick-up and drop-off coal traffic.

Below A wretchedly wet, decidedly chilly winter's day saw Fred and me bravely holding our ground on Grantham's windswept platforms. I had taken temporary refuge in the waiting room on the up platform and circulation was on its way back to my stiff fingers when Fred popped his head through the doorway to shout out excitedly, 'It's the "W1", it's on freight!' Blessed with very sharp eyes, he had read the smokebox number while still far off. Out we shot in time to catch our final view of this unique engine as it slowly chugged its way past us with a short freight. What a come-down, I thought, for what had once been a brave, highly adventurous experiment in the 1930s, then a barely successful rebuild. This was Fred's second shot of the erstwhile 'Hush-Hush' No 10000 in No 60700 format, for not so long before he had pedalled out, solo, to Peascliffe Tunnel, as much for the cycle ride as for the railway's delights. Out of the tunnel smoke had come the 'W1', its footplate a little overcrowded by the presence of special, immaculately-overalled observers. Fred's Voigtländer

shutter fired and captured the sedately moving engine. He was chuffed, naturally, just as I was later to get my own shot. My sole regret was that we had not been standing on the opposite platform from which our cameras could have recorded the unique wheel arrangement of 4-6-2-2.

Bottom Cameras were seized as a very noisy express was heard then seen passing under the distant road bridge over closed Brinklow station. Obviously a passenger express, but neither Fred nor I could discern what class of engine was in charge, for it resembled none of the passenger types we knew so well. When a mere quarter of a mile away it became apparent that it was a Stanier 8F 2-8-0. Unusual indeed, we thought, and promptly snapped it. Its lamp head-code implied an empty stock train, substantiated seconds later as we stared into completely empty carriages. We did not think, until too late, to count the coaches, for it was an inordinately lengthy train, but even so an attempt was made by staring up the line to count the disappearing front stock to add it on as

accurately as we could to what was still passing us. Somewhere in the region of nineteen coaches were behind that 2-8-0, the loco doubtless having been selected for its ability to haul heavy loads. It was no slouch either, for it roared past, its wee wheels wildly whizzing, at a more or less express passenger speed. Its raucous racket resounded for far longer than that of any express passenger train. What a sight, what sounds, what a magic, chemical odour, what an outpouring of tenacious power and, above all, what a footplate crew, the fireman in particular shovelling for all he was worth to maintain it. We had been enveloped for several minutes in an almost out-of-this-world mystery, but certainly a harmonic one.

Above 'Halls' were extremely common no matter where one went on the majority of GWR routes, so after securing enough snaps over the years they were allowed to steam past unphotographed. However, this lusciously sparkling example, in appealing BR lined-black mixed-traffic livery seduced the cameraman as it sauntered through Leamington Spa. The superb range of GWR signals was likewise too attractive to ignore.

Below Always on the look-out for engines redolent of the distant railway past, I was surprised to meet this round-top-boilered ex-Midland Railway 2F 0-6-0 at Burton-on-Trent. No 58236 had been a regular worker on the Leicester West Bridge to Coalville traffic. Not having seen her along that haunting route, I had assumed she was dead and dismembered, yet here she was, a wheezy, steam-leaking old dame heaving along a vast length of coal empties. It was lovely to wave 'hello' again to the footplate staff, assuming they were going to take the familiar Swannington-Leicester line!

Above Although the primary subject is the 'A1' sweeping down Stoke Bank, I chose to include the original GNR Castle Bytham signal box, the GNR anti-trespass board, the signals and, in particular, the distant girder bridge carrying the Midland & Great North Joint Railway line over the GNR track, all of which have since been swept away for ever.

Below 'V2' 2-6-2 No 60828 reveals the effort required to surmount Stoke Bank as it reaches the wooden inter-platform trolley-crossing at Castle Bytham. Once again, ancillaries are included: another GNR trespass warning board, point rodding, sidings, buffer stops and an LNER signal, atop a tall GNR lattice post – all gone now.

Above Working in Leicester Central carriage sheds occasionally allowed me privileged sightings when outside the structure. Lugging my bucket and brush, I was on my way from the sheds to the station to cover for an absent porter/cleaner. Stepping on to the permanent way, camera in my back pocket (couldn't miss a chance like this!) I had just a few seconds to pull it out and record *Faendre Hall* working her way back to home territory with an express fish train. The acridity of her exhaust was swiftly smothered by the sickly emanations from the fish-stuffed vans. I could smell it all the rest of the long way to the station, walking 'wrong line', of course, to face oncoming traffic.

Right Not far out from Leicester Belgrave Road station, the Great Northern line to Marefield Junction and beyond plunged into Ingarsby Tunnel. In the days when a regular, though sparse, service still ran, I and a friend cycled out to record the tunnel. Light engines and the occasional freight train rumbled through from time to time, and from their sound we could gauge how much time it took for a train to enter and leave the tunnel in the down direction. The 'tea-time train' of early Gresley stock (still in LNER teak livery) duly appeared behind its habitual 'J6'. Stepping into the tunnel after cocking our ears for a down train, we snatched our photos, mine framed by the arched portal. The driver of the 'J6' gave a friendly toot and a wave, and not the expected 'Get out of there!' yell and warning fist-flourish. Back on the embankment we sat for perhaps half a minute when a trainless 'J6' emerged, whistle blowing furiously; we suspected that the passenger train driver had communicated our risky presence to its driver in the tunnel. He also gave a wave, but made his admonishing point by vigorously shaking his head at us – a most definite negative sign indeed. We pedalled home very shortly afterwards, fearing that the railway police might have been informed.

Above A happy snap, for it comprises a portrait of a well-cleaned ex-GER 'D16' 4-4-0 and the eager mass of our school railway club members as we are about to leave Cambridge to descend on Ely shed. The tall sixth-former in the background is David Robinson, who was the skilful organiser of our considerable number of shed visits, which gave so much pleasure to so many over a few years. Where are you now, David?

Below Unusually 'at a loose end' one Saturday, I set off, solo, to pedal to Essendine, that once important junction, to see expresses running – sprinting! – down one of the fastest sections of Stoke Bank. Not many photos were taken, for the top shutter-speed on my camera was incapable of freezing motion of at least 90mph – one or two probably exceeding the magical 100. The only line still joining the main one came from Stamford. Hours went by and nothing appeared on it.

About to swing back into the saddle for a lengthy ride home, a few distant, desultory rings of smoke caused me to re-lean my cycle against the station wall. Far away something was on line from Stamford, certainly not a passenger train, for any of its travellers could have walked faster. Sensitive to my impatience, the train accelerated somewhat, eventually revealing itself to be a hugely long freight train, hauled most unsuitably by a GNR 'C12' 4-4-2T. No 67365 dated from 1898, a member of a class of around fifty fast suburban locomotives, a regular on the erstwhile passenger services between Stamford and Essendine. Only three other examples of the class exist in my collection – the station pilots at Grantham and Cambridge, and a scruffy shunter at the latter's yards. Graceful and of some historic importance, they would have made ideal engines to restore for working along preserved lines. Now there's an interesting 'new-build' project!

Above Two hours had been spent in dreadful weather in the GWR's Exeter St David's station. When the rain wandered off to drench folk elsewhere, I and my companion David pedalled up to see what was on offer at the ex-LSWR Queen Street station. Very little was going on. The sight of heavily braked trains descending to St David's – up to three engines – led us to expect similar sights of ascending trains. Not one 'West Country' came blasting her way up with hearty shovings from the rear. Patience was partly rewarded when a freight train roared up the incline. The pilot engine we had already met down below – an 'E1/R' (an 'E1' with trailing pony-truck). Behind her was an Ivatt 2-6-2T – no great novelty either, for one had been the station pilot for years at Leicester Midland. Nevertheless it made for an interesting photograph. To my chagrin, the banking engine(s?) dropped off well before the station portals, too far away to be recognised let alone photographed. That settled it! Off we pedalled to the next youth hostel after a happier hour in Exeter Cathedral, delighting in the choir.

Above right Waverley and Princes Street stations, Haymarket and Dalry Road shed having been 'done', Fred and I settled down for more restful photography in Princes Street Gardens, Edinburgh. Unending was the procession of trains and light engines for us to selectively photograph. Along with *Dumfries-shire* and *Peebles-shire*, *Inverness-shire* had to have the hyphenated spelling (not always employed in official documents, etc, by the way) to avoid the triple 'sss', which looked odd in the latter's case, and the double 'ss' in the former pair. Of course, today's regional re-organisation has solved the problem: 'Highland Region', 'Scottish Borders', and 'Dumfries & Galloway'.

'D49' No 62725 *Inverness-shire* makes an interesting shot for other reasons: she is hauling ex-North British Railway stock, while her tender is of former Great Central Railway parentage – probably from a withdrawn 'Scottish Director', Gresley's answer to the chronic shortage of motive power being to build more GCR 'Directors' to the Scottish loading gauge and make them acceptable by naming them after characters from Sir Walter Scott's novels (none of whom, being fictitious, could have been directors of the North British Railway, yet the name 'Scottish Directors' stuck, immovably, to the very end of their lives).

Above A scene that will live for ever in my mind was the welcoming sight of my return train to Durham from Sunderland. I was chilled to the core, starving hungry and possibly too late for the college evening meal. A wonder-filled day had been spent in and around Sunderland at the cost of nil sustenance, not even a cup of warming tea, for there had been so much to chase up, and exploration of the harbour had been exhaustive and thus exhausting. No 67321, one of those delightful 'G5' 0-4-4 tanks, made a lively run all the way with cracking starts from every station – normal practice – while her train-heating system worked wonders on my frozen frame.

Left Probably because the GWR diesel railcars had been introduced ages ago (1934-44), before nationalisation, they were never demonised by steam-lovers. Certainly they were far more attractive, visually, than the early BR railcars. This example is arriving at Monmouth (Troy) station from Chepstow.

Above Tempting providence with a top shutter speed of a mere 1/150th of a second on my 'Lumière' camera, I could not resist attempting to record this 'Jubilee' haring south near Sileby with a Manchester-St Pancras train. *Frobisher* was named after a famous admiral, as were thirty-nine others of the class, for the LMS had run out of member countries of the British Empire after which it could name further 'Jubilees'. When the naval worthies list was exhausted, the company resorted to naming the remainder of the class after sea battles and battleships, then, finally, three counties of Northern Ireland.

Below A lovely summery day brought us to the S&DJR terminus in Bridgwater in time to photograph a clean MR 3F due to set off, tender-first, with a set of sparkling coaches for – we believed – the Cheddar Valley line, though not before we had snapped it and also taken a close-up shot of its automatic tablet-changing apparatus. After its departure, Fred and I wandered back into some sunlight at the platform end. How lucky for us, for there we beheld this magnificent, original anti-trespass cast iron sign attached to a latticework signal post. Recently repainted in Southern Railway green, every letter looking as crisp and un-weathered as the day it was cast in or around 1903, it insisted on being photographed. What a near priceless relic today for those gullible enough to lash out vast sums on steam's bygone ancillary accoutrements!

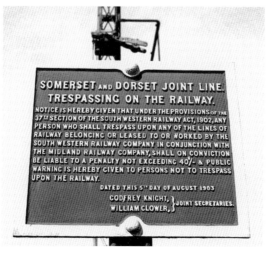

INDEX OF LOCATIONS